Hands-On Data Visualization with Bokeh

Interactive web plotting for Python using Bokeh

Kevin Jolly

BIRMINGHAM - MUMBAI

Hands-On Data Visualization with Bokeh

Commissioning Editor: Amey Varangaonkar
Acquisition Editor: Noyonika Das
Content Development Editor: Aditi Gour
Technical Editor: Jinesh Topiwala
Copy Editor: Safis Editing
Project Coordinator: Hardik Bhinde
Proofreader: Safis Editing
Indexer: Aishwarya Gangawane
Graphics: Jason Monteiro
Production Coordinator: Nilesh Mohite

First published: June 2018

Production reference: 1120618

Published by Packt Publishing Ltd.
Livery Place
35 Livery Street
Birmingham
B3 2PB, UK.

ISBN 978-1-78913-540-4

www.packtpub.com

This book is dedicated to my grandfather, P.J Mathai whose knowledge about the world sparked the flame of curiosity within me.

`mapt.io`

Mapt is an online digital library that gives you full access to over 5,000 books and videos, as well as industry leading tools to help you plan your personal development and advance your career. For more information, please visit our website.

Why subscribe?

- Spend less time learning and more time coding with practical eBooks and Videos from over 4,000 industry professionals

- Improve your learning with Skill Plans built especially for you

- Get a free eBook or video every month

- Mapt is fully searchable

- Copy and paste, print, and bookmark content

PacktPub.com

Did you know that Packt offers eBook versions of every book published, with PDF and ePub files available? You can upgrade to the eBook version at `www.PacktPub.com` and, as a print book customer, you are entitled to a discount on the eBook copy. Get in touch with us at `service@packtpub.com` for more details.

At `www.PacktPub.com`, you can also read a collection of free technical articles, sign up for a range of free newsletters, and receive exclusive discounts and offers on Packt books and eBooks.

Contributors

About the author

As a formally educated data scientist with a master's degree in data science from the prestigious King's College London, **Kevin** works as a data scientist with a digital healthcare startup - Connido Limited in London where he is primarily involved with building the descriptive, diagnostic and predictive analytic pipelines.

He is also the founder of LinearData—a leading online resource in the field of data science which has over 30,000 unique website hits.

About the reviewer

Zaim Awang, who is from Malaysia, has been an oil and gas engineer for more than 20 years—but a data scientist at heart for just as long. A graduate from the University of Texas in Austin, he used to work for Shell and other companies in different regions. He enjoys solving technical problems. His latest discovery is a new algorithm for pattern prediction that works much better than traditional deep learning for structured data. He is now leading a team at Invigour Energy developing AiSara (for solution approximation with robust algorithms). He welcomes contact at his twitter handle, @zaim_awang.

Packt is searching for authors like you

If you're interested in becoming an author for Packt, please visit authors.packtpub.com and apply today. We have worked with thousands of developers and tech professionals, just like you, to help them share their insights with the global tech community. You can make a general application, apply for a specific hot topic that we are recruiting an author for, or submit your own idea.

Table of Contents

Preface

Bokeh is an open source, interactive, data visualization package in Python that allows users to create interactive and beautiful visualizations that are both statistically significant and aesthetically pleasing.

This book aims to provide you with the tools needed to get started with Bokeh and to create plots that can tell a story through interaction.

Who this book is for

This book is well suited for data scientists and data analysts who wish to perform interactive data visualization on their web browsers using the Bokeh library.

A basic knowledge of Python is required in order to understand the content of this book.

What this book covers

Chapter 1, *Bokeh Installation and Key Concepts*, looks at how to install Bokeh on your PC and how to understand the fundamental concepts that are needed to progress with the rest of the book.

Chapter 2, *Plotting Using Glyphs*, will teach you how to create visualizations using the building block of Bokeh—Glyphs.

Chapter 3, *Plotting with Different Data Structures*, explains how to create visualizations using data structures that are found ubiquitously, such as the Pandas DataFrame and the NumPy array.

Chapter 4, *Using Layouts for Effective Presentation*, explores how to use layouts in order to enhance the aesthetic appeal of your visualizations.

Chapter 5, *Using Annotations, Widgets, and Visual Attributes for Visual Enhancement*, will teach you how to enhance your plot's interactivity as well as its aesthetics.

Chapter 6, *Building and Hosting Applications on the Bokeh Server*, goes through how to create and deploy applications that can host interactive visualizations.

Chapter 7, *Advanced Plotting with Networks, Geo Data, WebGL, and Exporting Plots*, dives into the advanced topics of Bokeh and sheds light on some of the ways in which you can enhance your interactive plotting experience.

Chapter 8, *The Bokeh Workflow – A Case Study*, comprises a case study that will have you explore data and build an interactive visualization by following a workflow that is tailored for Bokeh!

To get the most out of this book

A basic knowledge of Python is essential. Knowledge of importing packages, and experience of working with NumPy, Pandas, and DataFrames, will help the reader get the most out of this book.

Download the example code files

You can download the example code files for this book from your account at www.packtpub.com. If you purchased this book elsewhere, you can visit www.packtpub.com/support and register to have the files emailed directly to you.

You can download the code files by following these steps:

1. Log in or register at www.packtpub.com.
2. Select the **SUPPORT** tab.
3. Click on **Code Downloads & Errata**.
4. Enter the name of the book in the **Search** box and follow the onscreen instructions.

Once the file is downloaded, please make sure that you unzip or extract the folder using the latest version of:

- WinRAR/7-Zip for Windows
- Zipeg/iZip/UnRarX for Mac
- 7-Zip/PeaZip for Linux

The code bundle for the book is also hosted on GitHub at `https://github.com/PacktPublishing/Hands-on-Data-Visualization-with-Bokeh`. If there's an update to the code, it will be updated on the existing GitHub repository.

We also have other code bundles from our rich catalog of books and videos available at `https://github.com/PacktPublishing/`. Check them out!

Download the color images

We also provide a PDF file that has color images of the screenshots/diagrams used in this book. You can download it here: `https://www.packtpub.com/sites/default/files/downloads/Hands-onDataVisualizationwithBokeh_ColorImages.pdf`.

Code in action

Visit the following link to check out videos of the code being run:

`http://bit.ly/2xZJdHt`.

Conventions used

There are a number of text conventions used throughout this book.

`CodeInText`: Indicates code words in text, database table names, folder names, filenames, file extensions, pathnames, dummy URLs, user input, and Twitter handles. Here is an example: "We had to set the x-axis type to `datetime` in the `figure` function in order to render dates along the x-axis".

A block of code is set as follows:

```
#Output the plot

output_file('second_plot.html')

show(plot2)
```

Any command-line input or output is written as follows:

```
bokeh serve --show bokeh.py
```

Bold: Indicates a new term, an important word, or words that you see on screen. For example, words in menus or dialog boxes appear in the text in bold. Here is an example: "We will be working with the **S&P 500 stock data** found on Kaggle."

Warnings or important notes appear like this.

Tips and tricks appear like this.

Get in touch

Feedback from our readers is always welcome.

General feedback: Email feedback@packtpub.com and mention the book title in the subject of your message. If you have questions about any aspect of this book, please email us at questions@packtpub.com.

Errata: Although we have taken every care to ensure the accuracy of our content, mistakes do happen. If you have found a mistake in this book, we would be grateful if you would report this to us. Please visit www.packtpub.com/submit-errata, selecting your book, clicking on the Errata Submission Form link, and entering the details.

Piracy: If you come across any illegal copies of our works in any form on the internet, we would be grateful if you would provide us with the location address or website name. Please contact us at copyright@packtpub.com with a link to the material.

If you are interested in becoming an author: If there is a topic that you have expertise in and you are interested in either writing or contributing to a book, please visit authors.packtpub.com.

Reviews

Please leave a review. Once you have read and used this book, why not leave a review on the site that you purchased it from? Potential readers can then see and use your unbiased opinion to make purchase decisions, we at Packt can understand what you think about our products, and our authors can see your feedback on their book. Thank you!

For more information about Packt, please visit `packtpub.com`.

Bokeh Installation and Key Concepts

1

Welcome to the world of interactive data visualization using the popular Bokeh library in Python. As you go through the chapter, you will learn about the following topics:

- What exactly Bokeh is and how it differs from other plotting libraries
- How you can install Bokeh on your local machine
- How to verify your Bokeh installation
- Where you can go for help should things go wrong
- Some key concepts regarding Bokeh's internal workings

Bokeh is an interactive data visualization library in Python that helps users across all levels visualize both simple and complex data from datasets ranging from small to big. You can use Bokeh to create both interactive plots and applications that speak to the general public, statisticians, and even business leaders!

Technical requirements

You will be required to have Python installed on a system. Finally, to use the Git repository of this book, the user needs to install Git.

The code files of this chapter can be found on GitHub:
`https://github.com/PacktPublishing/Hands-on-Data-Visualization-with-Bokeh`.

Check out the following video to see the code in action:

`http://bit.ly/2l0d7Cb`.

The difference between static and interactive plotting

In the world of data visualization, there are three main libraries using Python that dominate the market, and these are as follows:

- Matplotlib
- Seaborn
- Bokeh

The first two, Matplotlib and Seaborn, let you plot static plots—plots that do not change and plots that cannot be interacted with. These plots are useful and add value when performing exploratory data analysis, as they are quick and easy to implement and very fast to execute.

The third plotting library, Bokeh, lets you plot interactive plots—plots that change when the user interacts with them. These plots are useful when you want to give your audience a wide range of options and tools for inferring and looking at data from various angles.

Installing the Bokeh library

Bokeh has a few dependencies. In order to use Bokeh, ensure that the following packages are already installed:

- NumPy
- Jinja2
- Six
- Requests
- Tornado >= 4.0
- PyYaml
- DateUtil

If you're using Python 2.7, ensure that you have all the afore mentioned packages along with:

- Futures

Installing Bokeh using a Python distribution

If you have all of your Python packages installed and managed using a distribution such as **Anaconda**, you can install Bokeh using your Bash Terminal or a Windows Prompt using the following code:

```
conda install bokeh
```

You can also install Bokeh using PyPi for Python 2 via the following code:

```
pip install bokeh
```

You can install Bokeh using PyPi for Python 3 via the following code:

```
pip3 install bokeh
```

For the purposes of this book, all plots will be rendered using Bokeh Version 0.12.15. If you already have Bokeh installed and require an update, simply enter the following code in your terminal or shell:

```
sudo pip3 install bokeh --upgrade
```

Verifying your installation

Once you have installed Bokeh, you will want to verify that it is correctly installed. In order to verify the installation and create all your Bokeh plots, you'll need a Jupyter Notebook. If you are not familiar with working with a Jupyter Notebook before or have installed, the following link will provide you with a step-by-step tutorial on how to install and work with Jupyter Notebook: http://jupyter.org/install.

You can verify your installation of Bokeh by generating a simple line plot using a Jupyter Notebook with the following code:

```
from bokeh.plotting import figure, output_file, show

#HTML file to output your plot into
output_file("bokeh.html")

#Constructing a basic line plot

x = [1,2,3]
y = [4,5,6]

p = figure()

p.line(x,y)

show(p)
```

This should open up a new tab on your browser with a plot illustrated as follows:

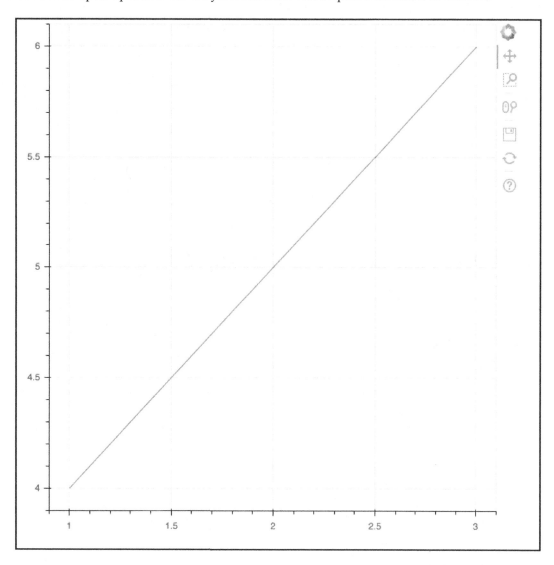

 Don't worry too much about what the code does for now. If you have got the preceding plot, you should be satisfied that Bokeh has been successfully installed on your local machine.

When things go wrong

In the event that things go wrong with your installation, you have the following two options:

- The Bokeh mailing list (`https://groups.google.com/a/anaconda.com/forum/#!forum/bokeh`) is a group on Google that posts questions and queries related to Bokeh, which are then answered by experts who use the package on a regular basis. Joining this group or looking through its frequently asked questions should help you find the answer to your solution.
- You can also submit an issue on the Bokeh GitHub issue tracker (`https://github.com/bokeh/bokeh/issues`); your issue will usually be solved in within a matter of a few hours, up to a few days.

Key concepts and the building blocks of Bokeh

While going through this book, you will come across some terms that are fundamental to understanding the Bokeh package. This section will take you through them.

The following are some key definitions related to Bokeh:

- **Application**: The Bokeh application is a rendered Bokeh document that runs in the browser
- **Glyphs**: Glyphs are the building blocks of Bokeh, and they are the lines, circles, rectangles, and other shapes that you see on a Bokeh plot
- **Server**: The Bokeh server is used to share and publish interactive plots and apps to an audience of your choice
- **Widgets**: Widgets in Bokeh are the sliders, drop-down menus, and other small tools that you can embed into your plot to add some interactivity

Plot outputs

There are two methods you can use to render your plot:

- output_file: This method is used to output your plot as an HTML file and can be used as illustrated in the following code:

```
output_file('plot.html')
```

- output_notebook: This is used to output your plot in the Jupyter Notebook you are presently working on and can be used as illustrated in the following code:

```
output_notebook()
```

Interfaces:

The first step to understanding interfaces is to understand what a class and a method are. Think of a class as a vessel that holds different types of cookie together. The vessel in this case is the class and the cookies are the methods that give the vessel some functionality, in our case, as a container for the cookies.

Since Python is an object-oriented programming language, it uses classes to group different objects that it creates together.

A class by itself is useless unless it has some functionality associated with it. These functionalities are provided to classes by methods.

Bokeh provides a mid-level plotting interface, similar to that of matplotlib , which is known as bokeh.plotting. The main class in the bokeh.plotting interface is the Figure class, which includes methods for adding different kinds of glyphs to a plot.

A user can create a Figure object by using the figure function, as illustrated in the following code:

```
from bokeh.plotting import figure

# create a Figure object
p = figure(plot_width=500, plot_height=400, tools="pan,hover")
```

In Bokeh, the figure function, as illustrated in the preceding code, is used to initialize and store the contents of your plot. The variable *p* in the preceding code now holds information about the plot, including its height, width, and the kind of tools the plot will use.
Since figure is our main class, methods such as line, circle, and so on can be added to our diagram in order to create the plot.

Summary

This chapter has given you the exact set of steps required for installing Bokeh on your local machine. It has also given you a glimpse of the key terms that you'll run into as you work your way through this book.

Now that Bokeh has been successfully installed on your local machine, you can open up a new Jupyter Notebook to work on your first plots with Bokeh!

In the next chapter, you will learn how to create your very first plot using glyphs; you'll see how it lays the foundation for plotting using Bokeh.

2
Plotting using Glyphs

Glyphs are the fundamental building blocks of Bokeh and are used to create a wide variety of plots. In fact, every single plot that you build while working with Bokeh has a glyph mechanism attached to it, such as lines, rectangles, circles, and any other object that makes up the plot.

In this chapter, you will learn about the following topics:

- What glyphs are
- How you can plot with glyphs
- How to create scatter plots using glyphs
- How you can customize glyphs

Technical requirements

You will be required to have Python installed on a system. Finally, to use the Git repository of this book, the user needs to install Git.

The code files of this chapter can be found on GitHub:
https://github.com/PacktPublishing/Hands-on-Data-Visualization-with-Bokeh.

Check out the following video to see the code in action:

http://bit.ly/2sMGWdU.

What are glyphs?

When you see a plot, interactive or not, it is usually composed of geometric shapes that make up every element in that plot. In Bokeh, these geometric shapes are called glyphs. If we wanted to create a line plot, we would have to use a **line** to represent information on the plot, and if we wanted to create a scatter plot with a circle as our marker, we would use a **circle** to represent that information.

These geometric shapes that are used to convey visual information to readers about a piece of data are called glyphs.

In this book, we will help you plot the four types of plot where above using glyphs, and we will also give you information on the various types of plot that can be plotted using glyphs.

Plotting with glyphs

In this section, we will learn how to plot the following types of plot using glyphs:

- **Line plots**: Line plots offer a way of visualizing the movements of points along the *x*-and *y*-axes in the form of a line. These plots are useful for performing time series analytics.
- **Bar plots**: Bar plots are useful for indicating the count of each category of a particular column or field in your dataset.
- **Patch plots**: Patch plots are used to indicate a region of points in a particular shade of color. Such plots can be used to distinguish different groups within the same dataset.
- **Scatter plots**: Scatter plots are used to visualize the relationship between two variables and to indicate the strength of correlation between them.

Creating line plots

We can plot a simple line plot in Bokeh using the following code:

```
#Importing the required packages

from bokeh.io import output_file, show

from bokeh.plotting import figure

#Creating our data arrays used for plotting the line plot

x = [5,6,7,8,9,10]

y = [1,2,3,4,5,6]

#Calling the figure() function to create the figure of the plot

plot = figure()

#Creating a line plot using the line() function

plot.line(x,y)

#Creating markers on our line plot at the location of the intersection
between x and y

plot.cross(x,y, size = 15)

#Output the plot

output_file('line_plot.html')

show(plot)
```

This results in a plot illustrated as follows:

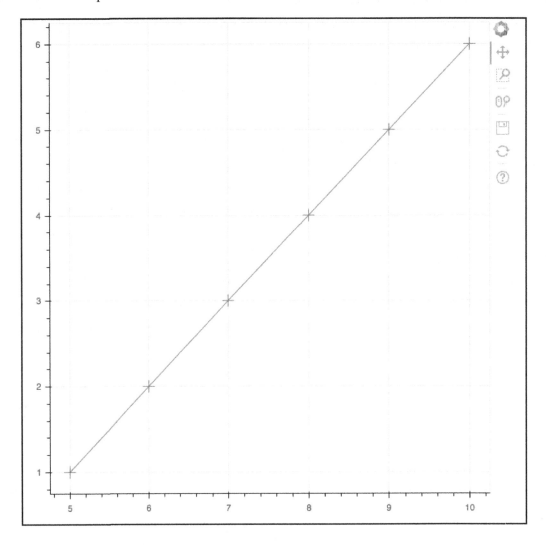

In the preceding code, we first called the `figure()` function as a way to instruct Bokeh to construct a diagram. Once we've done this, we can then add layers of glyphs or geometric shapes to our diagram.

We first added the `line()` glyph to the figure in order to construct the line plot and then added the `cross()` glyph on top of the line to mark intersections between the *x* and *y* points.

Creating bar plots

Now let's take a look at constructing a simple bar plot. We can do this using the following code:

```
#Importing the required packages

from bokeh.plotting import figure, show, output_file

#Points on the x axis

x = [8,9,10]

#Points on the y axis

y = [1,2,3]

#Creating the figure of the plot

plot = figure()

#Code to create the barplot

plot.vbar(x,top = y, color = "blue", width= 0.5)

#Output the plot

output_file('barplot.html')

show(plot)
```

This results in a plot illustrated as follows:

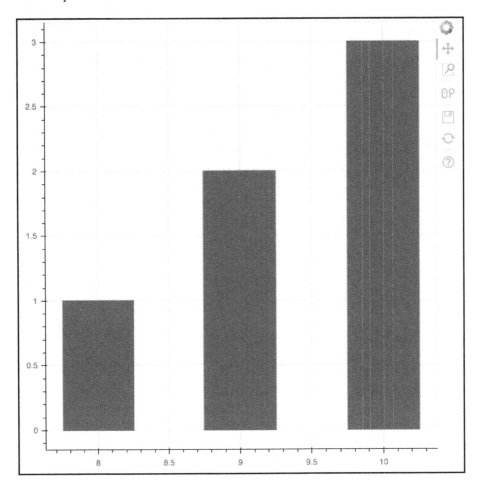

In the preceding code, we used the vbar, or the vertical bar function, to generate the bar plot. This takes in four arguments, the points along the *x*-axis: the **top** argument, the points along the *y*-axis, the color argument to give your plot a color of your choice, and the width argument, which you would want to set to 0.5 or 1 depending on the level of separation you'd like between your bars. Additionally, you can construct horizontal bar plots using the hbar function.

Creating patch plots

A patch plot shades a region of space in a particular color to indicate a region or a group having similar properties. We can construct a simple patch plot using the following code:

```
#Importing the required packages

from bokeh.io import output_file, show

from bokeh.plotting import figure

#Creating the regions to map

x_region = [[1,1,2,], [2,2,3], [2,3,5,4]]

y_region = [[2,5,6], [3,6,7], [2,4,7,8]]

#Creating the figure

plot = figure()

#Building the patch plot

plot.patches(x_region, y_region, fill_color = ['yellow', 'black', 'green'],
line_color = 'white')

#Output the plot

output_file('patch_plot.html')

show(plot)
```

This results in a plot illustrated as follows:

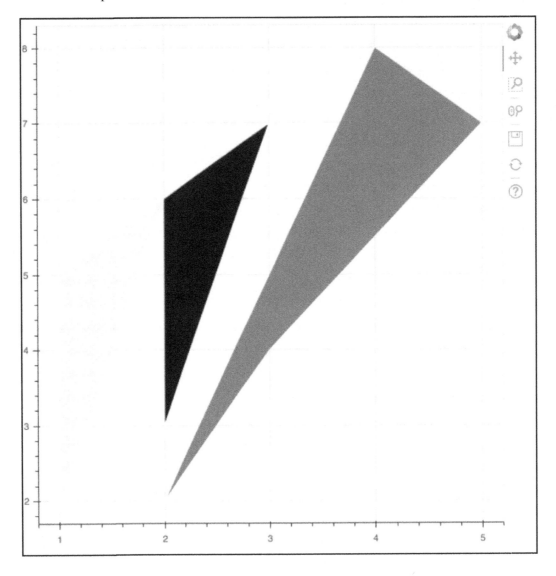

In the preceding code, the x_region and y_region were divided into three distinct regions. The first region of [1,1,2] along the *x*-axis maps the corresponding region of [2,5,6] along the *y*-axis and is given the color yellow. The second region of [2,2,3] along the *x*-axis maps the corresponding region of [3,6,7] along the *y*-axis and is given the color black. The third region of [2,3,5,4] along the *x*-axis maps the corresponding region of [2,4,7,8] along the *y*-axis and is given the color green. We then use the patches function to build the plot by giving it regions, along with the colors for each region as arguments. The line_color argument is used to give a border color to each of the patches.

Creating scatter plots

Scatter plots are one of the most commonly used plots to determine the bi-variate relationship between two variables, and as such are enhanced when we add interactivity to them using Bokeh. In order to construct a simple scatter plot using Bokeh, we can use the following code:

```
#Importing the required packages

from bokeh.io import output_file, show

from bokeh.plotting import figure

#Creating the figure

plot = figure()

#Creating the x and y points

x = [1,2,3,4,5]

y = [5,7,2,2,4]

#Plotting the points with a cirle marker

plot.circle(x,y, size = 30)

#Output the plot

output_file('scatter.html')

show(plot)
```

This results in a plot illustrated as follows:

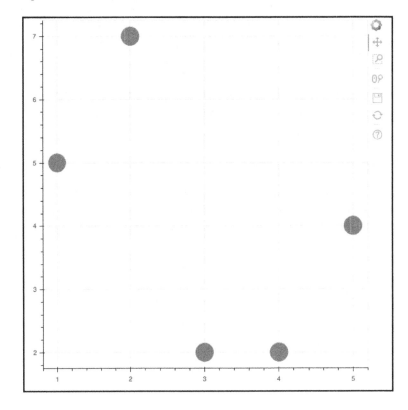

In the preceding code, we used the circle marker to create the scatter plot with a size of 30 for each of the circles. The circles represent the intersections between the points in the *x* and *y* lists.

Customizing glyphs

When creating the preceding scatter plot, we used the circle marker to indicate the points on the plot. Bokeh provides us with a wide variety of markers that you can use instead of the circle, and they are as follows:

```
- cross()
- x()
- diamond()
- diamond_cross()
```

```
- circle_x()
- circle_cross()
- triangle()
- inverted_triangle()
- square()
- square_x()
- square_cross()
- asterisk()
```

You can also add labels to the x-and y-axes by using the following code:

```
plot.figure(x_axis_label = "Label name of x axis", y_axis_label = "Label
name of y axis")
```

You can customize the transparency of the points on a scatter plot by using the following code:

```
plot.circle(x, y, alpha = 0.5)
```

The alpha argument takes in a range of values between 0 to 1, with 0 being completely transparent and 1 being opaque.

Summary

This chapter has given you an introduction to what glyphs are and how you can use them to create fundamental plots using Bokeh. We also looked at how to customize these plots further.

Glyphs are the fundamental building blocks of Bokeh and are required in order to create more complex, and statistically significant, plots in the future.

In this chapter, you learned how to create four different plots using glyphs. Line plots are commonly used in time series analytics, bar plots are commonly used to compare counts between different categories, patch plots are commonly used to highlight an area of points, and scatter plots, are commonly used to map a relationship between two or more variables.

In the upcoming chapter, we will take these concepts and use them to plot diagrams using NumPy arrays and Pandas DataFrames.

3
Plotting with different Data Structures

Now that you have learned how to build a visualization from scratch using Glyphs, we can extend this concept and construct plots using data structures such as the NumPy array and pandas DataFrame.

This chapter will also teach you about the `ColumnDataSource`, the core essence of the Bokeh library, which will allow you to share your data over multiple plots and widgets!

In a nutshell, you will get hands-on experience of using Bokeh with various data structures, as this chapter will take you through:

- Creating plots using NumPy arrays
- Creating plots with pandas DataFrames
- Creating plots using the `ColumnDataSource`

Technical requirements

You will be required to have Python installed on a system. Finally, to use the Git repository of this book, the user needs to install Git.

The code files of this chapter can be found on GitHub:
`https://github.com/PacktPublishing/Hands-on-Data-Visualization-with-Bokeh.`

Check out the following video to see the code in action:

`http://bit.ly/2MjrvSm.`

Creating plots using NumPy arrays

NumPy arrays are one of the most fundamental data structures found in Python and as such are an important data structure when it comes to creating interactive visualizations in Bokeh. In this section, we will cover how you can build line and scatter plots using NumPy arrays.

Creating line plots using NumPy arrays

In order to create a simple line plot using a NumPy array, we can use this code:

```
#Import required packages

import numpy as np
import random
from bokeh.io import output_file, show
from bokeh.plotting import figure

#Creating an array for the points along the x and y axes

array_x =np.array([1,2,3,4,5,6])

array_y = np.array([5,6,7,8,9,10])

#Creating a line plot

plot = figure()

plot.line(array_x, array_y)

#Output the plot

output_file('numpy_line.html')

show(plot)
```

This renders a plot as illustrated here:

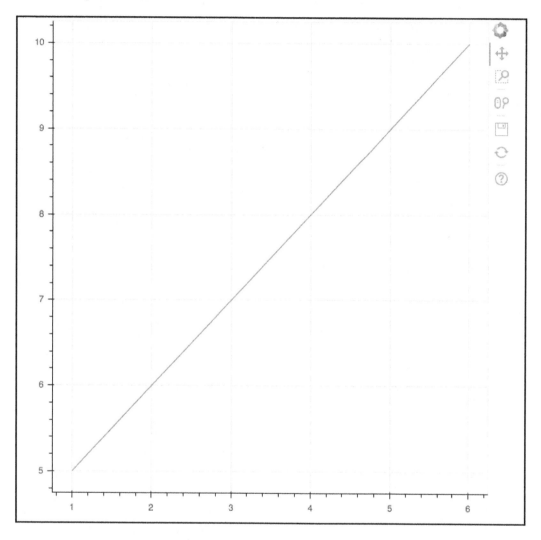

In the previous code, we created two NumPy arrays to hold the points along the *x*-and *y*-axes. We then used the regular Bokeh function calls that we learned about in the previous chapter with Glyphs to construct the line plot.

Creating scatter plots using NumPy arrays

In order to create a scatter plot using a NumPy array, we use the code shown here:

```
#Import required packages

import numpy as np
import random
from bokeh.io import output_file, show
from bokeh.plotting import figure

#Creating arrays for two different categories of points

x_red = np.array([1,2,3,4,5])
y_red = np.array([5,6,7,8,9])

x_blue = np.array([10,11,12,13])
y_blue = np.array([14,15,16,17])

#Creating the categorical scatter plot

plot = figure()

plot.circle(x_red, y_red, size = 9, color = 'red', alpha = 0.8)
plot.circle(x_blue, y_blue, size = 9, color = 'blue', alpha = 0.8)

#Output the plot

output_file('numpy_scatter.html')

show(plot)
```

This results in a plot as illustrated here:

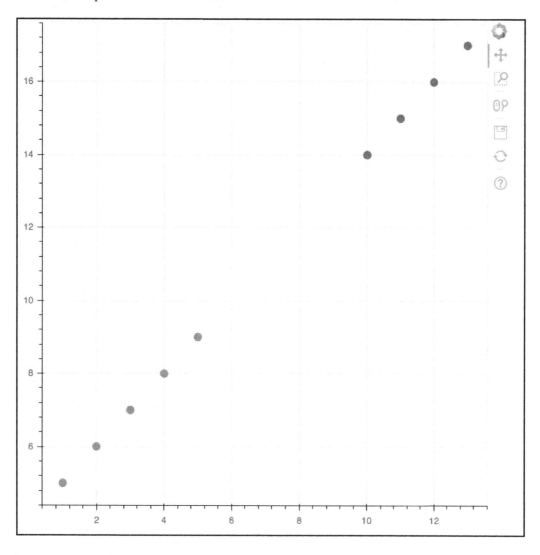

In the previous code, we created two distinct groups of points: a red group and a blue group. Each group had its own set of *x* and *y* points, which are NumPy arrays. We then created a scatter plot by coloring each group accordingly.

You can now see two distinct sets of colored points on your scatter plot. These plots are useful for visualizing categorical data.

Creating plots using pandas DataFrames

Most of the data that you will work with will be available in the CSV or Excel formats and thus you will inevitably convert them into a pandas DataFrame in order to work with them effectively. Bokeh extends its functionality to help us build interactive yet meaningful plots using a pandas DataFrame in Python. In this section, we will construct scatter plots and time series plots using a pandas DataFrame.

For this section, we will be using a popular dataset about the stock market found on Kaggle that can be accessed via this link: Kaggle **S&P 500 stock data** (https://www.kaggle.com/camnugent/sandp500/data).

As a first step, let's load the dataset into Jupyter Notebook. We can do this using the code shown here:

```
#Importing the required packages

import pandas as pd

#Read in the data

df = pd.read_csv('all_stocks_5yr.csv')

#Filtering for apple stocks

df_apple = df[df['Name'] == 'AAL']

#Converting the date column to a time series

df_apple['date'] = pd.to_datetime(df_apple['date'])
```

In the previous code, I saved the file I downloaded from Kaggle as all_stocks_5yr.csv and loaded it into Jupyter Notebook using pandas. I then filtered the stocks and created a new DataFrame with stock information about Apple only.

Creating a time series plot using a pandas DataFrame

A time series plot shows how points in a data set vary across a certain period of time. The time is usually plotted along the *x*-axis while the points of interest are on the *y*-axis.

We will now create a time series plot in order to visualize how the High Prices of the Apple stock vary across a 5-year period by using the code shown here:

```
#Import the required packages

from bokeh.io import output_file, show
from bokeh.plotting import figure
import pandas as pd

#Read in the data

df = pd.read_csv('all_stocks_5yr.csv')

#Filtering for apple stocks

df_apple = df[df['Name'] == 'AAL']

#Converting the date column to a time series

df_apple['date'] = pd.to_datetime(df_apple['date'])

#Create the time series plot

plot = figure(x_axis_type = 'datetime', x_axis_label = 'date', y_axis_label
= 'High Prices')

plot.line(x = df_apple['date'], y = df_apple['high'])

#Output the plot

output_file('pandas_time.html')

show(plot)
```

This results in a plot as illustrated here:

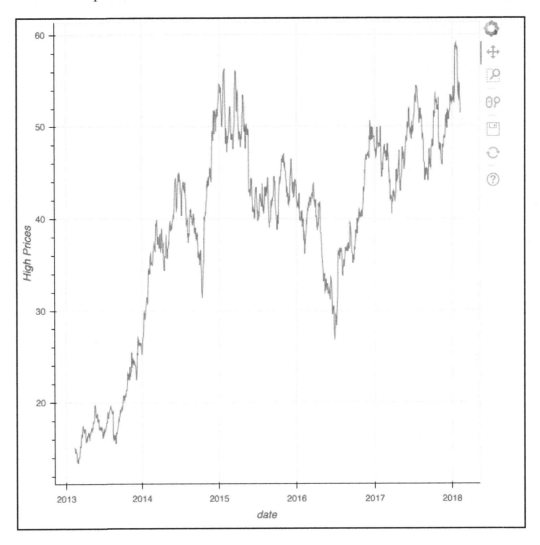

In the previous code, we had to set the *x*-axis type to `datetime` in the `figure` function in order to render dates along the *x*-axis. We then used the line function to generate a time series plot between the date and the high prices for Apple over the last 5-years.

Creating scatter plots using a pandas DataFrame

In order to create a scatter plot between the low and high prices, along with the opening and closing prices rendered in the same plot, we use the code shown here:

```
#Import the required packages

from bokeh.io import output_file, show
from bokeh.plotting import figure

#Create the scatter plot

plot = figure()

plot.circle(x = df_apple['high'], y = df_apple['low'], color = 'red', size
= 10, alpha = 0.8)

plot.diamond(x = df_apple['open'], y = df_apple['close'], color = 'green',
size = 10, alpha = 0.8)


#Output the plot

output_file('pandas_scatter.html')

show(plot)
```

This results in a plot as illustrated here:

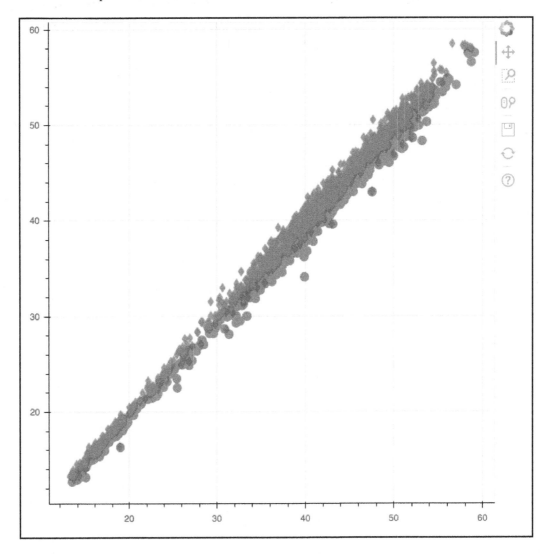

In the previous plot, the red circles represent the relationship between the high and low prices for Apple, while the green diamonds represent the relationship between the opening and closing prices. We used the `circle` function to create the red circles between the high and low prices, while we used the `diamond` function to create the green diamonds between the opening and closing prices.

Creating plots with ColumnDataSource

The `ColumnDataSource` provides us with a way to use the same data across multiple plots and widgets. By feeding data into the `ColumnDataSource`, you build a foundation of data that can be called upon whenever you please, instead of loading the data into your Jupyter Notebook multiple times.

Fundamentally, the `ColumnDataSource` creates a dictionary in which the value is the data contained in the column and the key is a string name that you specify for that particular column.

Creating a time series plot using the ColumnDataSource

In order to construct a time series plot using the `ColumnDataSource`, we use this code:

```
#Import the required packages

from bokeh.io import output_file, show
from bokeh.plotting import figure
from bokeh.plotting import ColumnDataSource

#Create the ColumnDataSource object

data = ColumnDataSource(df_apple)

#Create the time series plot

plot = figure(x_axis_type = 'datetime', x_axis_label = 'date', y_axis_label
= 'High Prices')

plot.line(x = 'date', y = 'high', source = data, color = 'red')

plot.circle(x = 'date', y = 'high', source = data, fill_color = 'white',
size = 3)

#Output the plot

output_file('CDS_time.html')

show(plot)
```

This results in a plot as illustrated here:

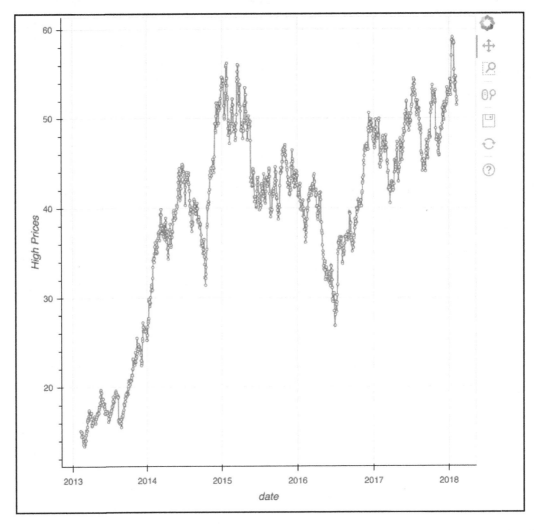

The plot shows us how the high prices of Apple's stock varied over a 5-year period with the blue circles indicating each price point of the stock.

When creating this plot, we passed the entire Apple stock DataFrame into the `ColumnDataSource` function and saved it into a variable called `data`.

We then used the source argument when creating the plot and passed in this data. We can now use the column names directly when creating the plot instead of calling the DataFrame.

Finally, we used the circle function to generate the blue circles with a white fill to represent the individual data points.

Creating a scatter plot using the ColumnDataSource

Another way to use the ColumnDataSource is to pass in data as shown in this code:

```
#Import the required packages

from bokeh.io import output_file, show
from bokeh.plotting import figure
from bokeh.models import ColumnDataSource


#Create the ColumnDataSource object

data = ColumnDataSource(data = {
    'x' : df_apple['high'],
    'y' : df_apple['low'],
    'x1': df_apple['open'],
    'x2': df_apple['close'],
})


#Create the scatter plot

plot = figure()

plot.cross(x = 'x', y = 'y', source = data, color = 'red', size = 10, alpha
= 0.8)

plot.circle(x = 'x1', y = 'x2', source = data, color = 'green', size = 10,
alpha = 0.3)

#Output the plot

output_file('CDS_scatter.html')

show(plot)
```

This results in a plot as illustrated here:

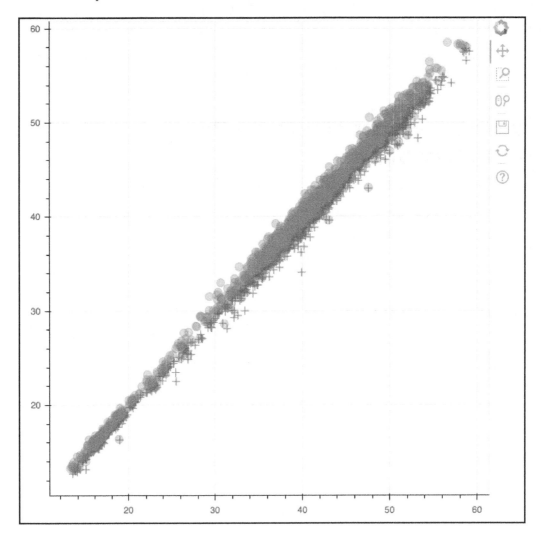

In the previous code, we mapped the columns of the DataFrame that we wanted to plot as the values in a dictionary consisting of key value pairs, with the keys being a string name of your choice and the value being the columns of the DataFrame.

We then passed this dictionary as the value for the data argument of the ColumnDataSource function. Finally, the keys of the dictionary were passed into the x and y arguments while creating the circle and cross scatter plots.

Summary

This chapter gave you an introduction to the most common data formats that you will encounter while working with Python, and how you can create visualizations in Bokeh using these formats.

You also learned about using the `ColumnDataSource` to map the column names to a list of data values that can be used across multiple plots and widgets.

In the upcoming chapter, you will learn about how you can use layouts for effective presentation of data using plots built from pandas DataFrames.

4
Using Layouts for Effective Presentation

While plotting multiple plots, it is always best to make use of layouts in order to display the plots side by side, or vertically on top of each other, in order to make statistical comparisons between the two plots and make them visually appealing at the same time.

The use of layouts, tabs, and grids effectively while creating plots with Bokeh will also allow you to link multiple plots together by making use of the same axes. This makes the comparison of multiple plots much more accurate than if you were to create the plots in separate cells in your Jupyter Notebook.

In this chapter, you will learn how to:

- Create multiple plots along the same row
- Create multiple plots along the same column
- Create multiple plots in a row and column
- Create multiple plots using a tabbed layout
- Create a robust grid layout
- Link multiple plots together

Technical requirements

You will be required to have Python installed on a system. Finally, to use the Git repository of this book, the user needs to install Git.

The code files of this chapter can be found on GitHub:
`https://github.com/PacktPublishing/Hands-on-Data-Visualization-with-Bokeh`.

Check out the following video to see the code in action:

`http://bit.ly/2sOMTab`.

Creating multiple plots along the same row

In order to create multiple plots along the same row, let's first create three unique plots. We will be working with the **S&P 500 stock data** found on Kaggle (`https://www.kaggle.com/camnugent/sandp500/data`).

The first step is to read the data and filter it so that we only use the data related to Apple as shown here:

```
#Import the required packages

import pandas as pd

#Read in the data

df = pd.read_csv('all_stocks_5yr.csv')

#Convert the date column into datetime data type

df['date'] = pd.to_datetime(df['date'])

#Filter the data for Apple stocks only

df_apple = df[df['Name'] == 'AAL']
```

Next, let's construct three unique plots using the code as shown here:

```
#Import the required packages

from bokeh.io import output_file, show
from bokeh.plotting import figure
from bokeh.plotting import ColumnDataSource
```

```
#Create the ColumnDataSource object

data = ColumnDataSource(data = {
    'x' : df_apple['high'],
    'y' : df_apple['low'],
    'x1': df_apple['open'],
    'y1': df_apple['close'],
    'x2': df_apple['date'],
    'y2': df_apple['volume'],
})


#Create the first scatter plot

plot1 = figure()

plot1.cross(x = 'x', y = 'y', source = data, color = 'red', size = 10,
alpha = 0.8)

#Create the second scatter plot

plot2 = figure()

plot2.circle(x = 'x1', y = 'y1', source = data, color = 'green', size = 10,
alpha = 0.3)

#Create the third scatter plot

plot3 = figure(x_axis_type = 'datetime', x_axis_label = 'date',
y_axis_label = 'Volume Traded')

plot3.line(x = 'x2', y = 'y2', source = data, color = 'red')

plot3.circle(x = 'x2', y = 'y2', source = data, fill_color = 'white', size
= 3)
```

In the previous code, we have created a `ColumnDataSource` object in order to map all the variables of interest.

The first scatter plot is between the high and low prices of Apple and can be displayed using the code shown here:

```
#Output the plot

output_file('first_plot.html')

show(plot1)
```

This results in a plot as illustrated here:

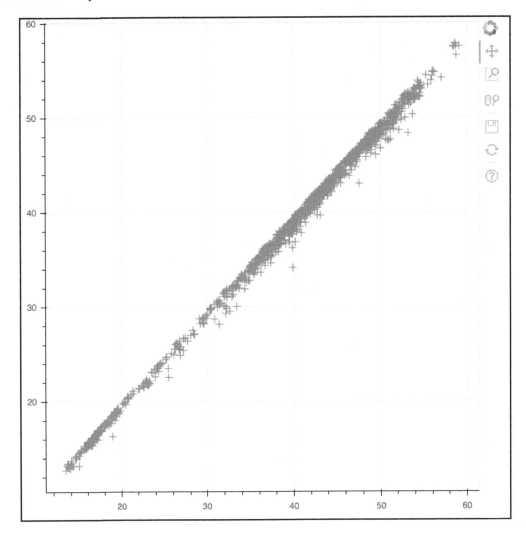

The second plot is between the opening and closing prices of Apple and can be displayed using this code:

```
#Output the plot

output_file('second_plot.html')

show(plot2)
```

This results in a plot as illustrated here:

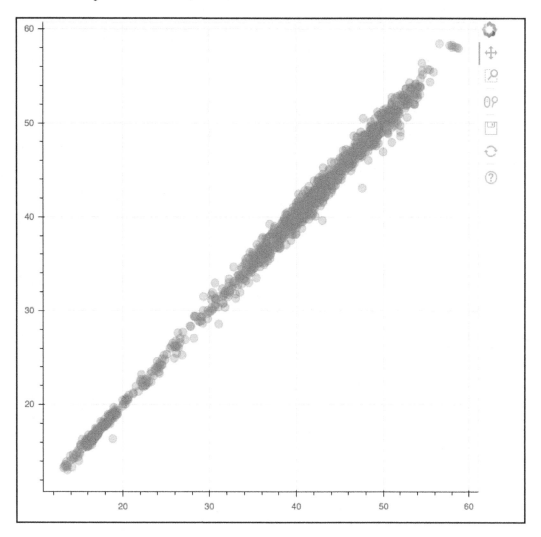

The third plot is a time series plot between the volume of Apple stocks traded over a 5-year period. We can display this plot using the code shown here:

```
#Output the plot

output_file('third_plot.html')

show(plot3)
```

This results in a plot as illustrated here:

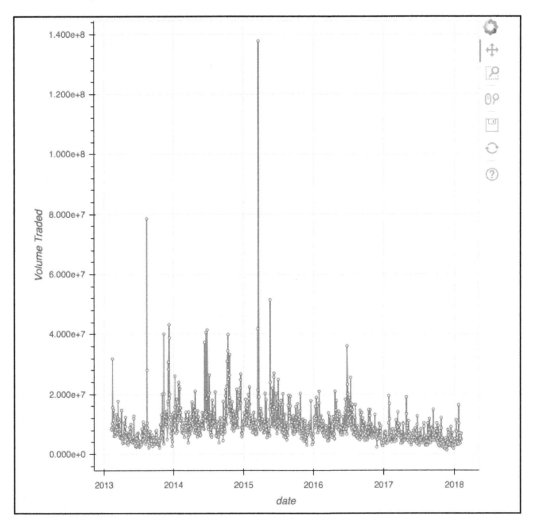

Notice how we have to create three separate outputs in order to view the three plots. This does not work to our advantage when we want to view the three plots side by side for quick and easy comparison of all three plots.

In order to plot the three plots in a horizontal row, we use the code as shown here:

```
#Import the required packages

from bokeh.layouts import row
from bokeh.io import output_file, show

#Group the 3 plots into a 'row' layout

row_layout = row(plot1,plot2,plot3)

#Output the plot

output_file('horizontal.html')

show(row_layout)
```

This results in a plot as illustrated here:

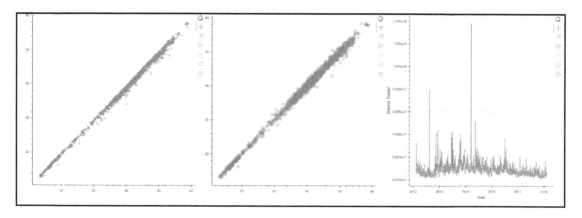

Plots 1, 2, and 3 in a horizontal layout

We can now observe that the three plots are stacked together side by side in a horizontal fashion. In the previous code, we made use of the *row* function, which takes in the plots that we created earlier as arguments in order to plot the three figures horizontally.

Creating multiple plots in the same column

In this section, you will learn how to stack multiple plots vertically on top of each other to create a column-wise comparison of plots. We will be using the two scatter plots that we created earlier in the chapter to achieve this.

In order to create a vertical layout of plots, we use the code shown here:

```
#Import the required packages

from bokeh.layouts import column
from bokeh.io import output_file, show

#Group the 2 plots into a 'column' layout

col_layout = column(plot1,plot2)

#Output the plot

output_file('vertical.html')

show(col_layout)
```

This results in a layout of plots, as illustrated here:

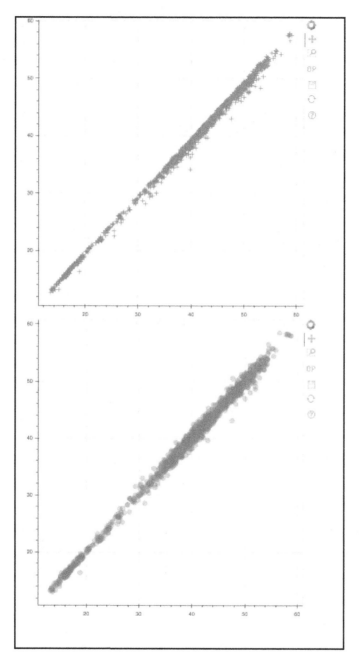

Plots 1 and 2 in a vertical layout

In the previous code, we used the `column` function, which takes in the plots that we want to stack vertically on top of each other as input arguments to create the vertical layout of plots. This creates a vertical layout of scatter plots that we can now use to compare.

Creating multiple plots in a row and column

We might see a situation in which we would like to compare the two scatter plots horizontally, but would like the time series plot to be stacked here with the scatter plots, but all within the embrace of the same layout.

Such a combination of horizontal and vertical layouts is called a nested layout.

We can construct a nested layout by using the code shown here:

```
#Import the required packages

from bokeh.layouts import column, row
from bokeh.io import output_file, show

#Construct the nested layout

nested_layout = column(row(plot1,plot2), plot3)

#Output the plot

output_file('nested.html')

show(nested_layout)
```

This results in a plot as illustrated here:

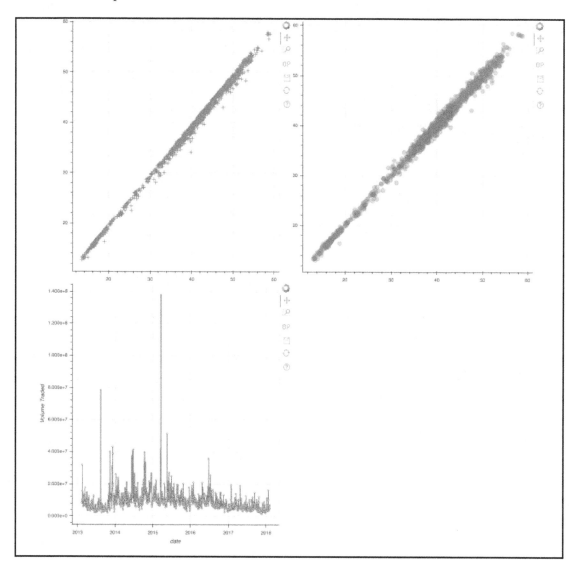

Plots 1, 2, and 3 in a nested layout

In the previous code, we used the row function to combine Plot 1 and Plot 2 in a horizontal row and then used the column function on the horizontal combination of the scatter plots and Plot 3.

This generated a nested layout with the scatter plots side by side while the time series plot was a separate entity here. Nested layouts provide an effective way to categorize certain groups of plots into rows and columns, and thus help us make sense of the data by enabling effective comparison.

Creating multiple plots using a tabbed layout

Sometimes it may be more effective to view a single plot at a time but have multiple plots in the same space. This can be done by making use of the tabbed layout that Bokeh offers. Using a tabbed layout, each plot is stored in a single tab and can be accessed by simply clicking on that tab.

We are going to use the same three plots as in the earlier sections to construct the tabbed layout.

In order to create plots in a tabbed layout, we can use the code shown here:

```
#Import the required packages

from bokeh.models.widgets import Tabs, Panel
from bokeh.io import output_file, show
from bokeh.layouts import column, row

#Create the two panels

tab1 = Panel(child = plot1, title = 'Tab One')

tab2 = Panel(child = column(plot2,plot3), title = 'Tab Two')

#Feed the tabs into a Tabs object

tabs_object = Tabs(tabs = [tab1, tab2])

#Output the plot

output_file('tab_layout.html')

show(tabs_object)
```

This results in a tabbed layout as illustrated here:

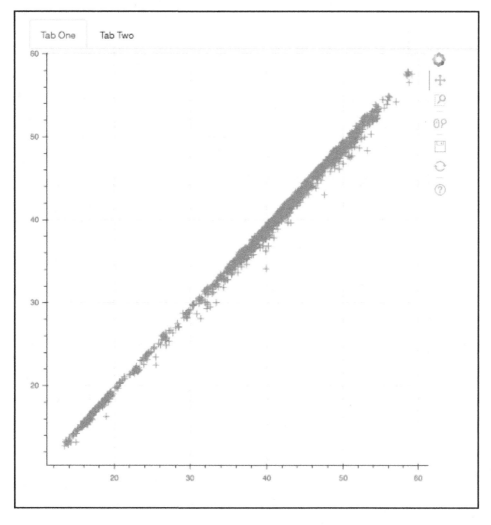

Plot 1 in a tabbed layout

In the previous code, we first created two panels using the `Panel` function. Each panel was made up its own set of plots, which was specified by using the `child` argument within the `Panel` function.

We then created a tabs object by using the `Tabs` function by passing in the panels to the `tabs` argument.

In the previous plot, we are presently on **Tab One**, which consists of a single scatter plot. If we click **Tab Two**, we will see Plot 2 and Plot 3 in a vertical layout as illustrated here:

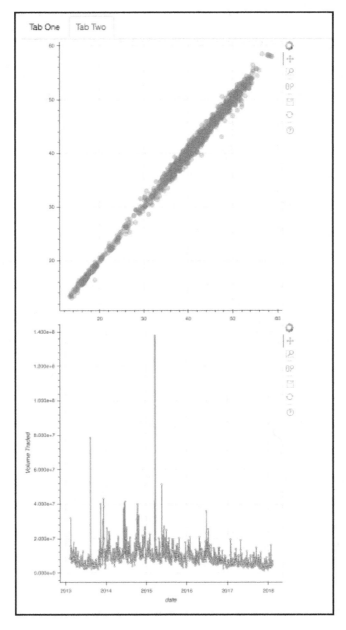

Plot 2 and Plot 3 in a vertical layout

Using tabbed layouts can be highly effective in cases where we want the ease of having all the plots in one place but at the same time want to view a single plot or a group of plots isolated without having all our plots cluttering the screen.

Creating a robust grid layout

A grid layout combines the row, column, and nested layouts, and allows you to create plots horizontally, vertically, or both horizontally and vertically. Using the grid layout is much more robust because of the versatility of combinations that the layout offers in terms of stacking multiple plots together in a single screen.

In order to construct a grid layout, we will use the same three plots that we have been working on in the previous sections.

We can create a nested grid layout using the code shown here:

```
#Import required packages

from bokeh.io import output_file, show
from bokeh.layouts import gridplot

#Create the grid layout

grid_layout = gridplot([plot1, plot2], [plot3, None])

#Output the plot

output_file('grid.html')

show(grid_layout)
```

This results in a grid layout as illustrated here:

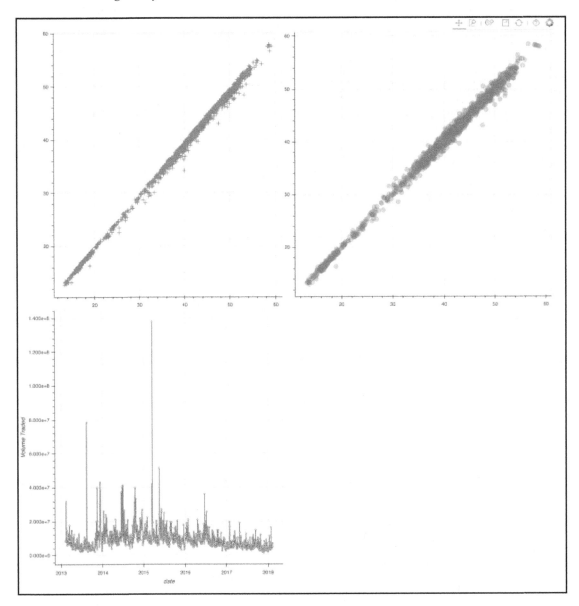

Creating a nested layout using the grid layout

In the previous code, we used the `gridplot` function to create the grid of plots as illustrated before. We passed in `plot1` and `plot2` as a list into the `gridplot` function, to indicate that we wanted `plot 1` and `plot2` displayed horizontally in the first row. We then passed in `plot3` and `None` as the second list to the `gridplot` function to indicate that we wanted `plot3` and no plot displayed horizontally in the second row.

Linking multiple plots together

At times, we might want our plots to have the same range of values along the *x*-and/or *y*-axes in order to facilitate meaningful comparison of the same range of points across different plots.

We will be working with `plot1`, `plot2`, and `plot3` as illustrated in the sections before this.

In order to create multiple plots with the same range along the *y*-axis, we use the code shown here:

```
#Import the required packages

from bokeh.io import output_file, show
from bokeh.layouts import row

#Creating equal y axis ranges

plot3.y_range = plot1.y_range

#Create the row layout

row_layout = row(plot3, plot1)

#Output the plot

output_file('grid.html')

show(row_layout)
```

This results in a layout of plots as illustrated here:

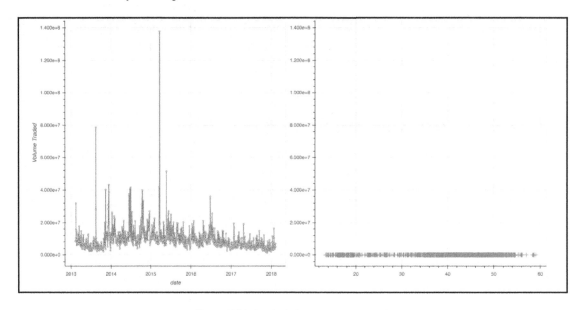

Plots 1 and 3 linked together by the same *y* axis range as plot 3

In the previous code, we gave `plot1` the same *y*-range as `plot3`. In the resulting chart, you can observe how `plot3` and `plot1` have the exact same *y*-axis ranges. You can also see that with `plot1`, initially a very linear scatter plot has become a horizontal line due to the change in its *y* axis range. This is because `plot1`'s initial *y*-axis range was between 0 and 60, but now that it takes on `plot3`'s *y*-axis range, which is a value in the range of 10^7, the plot's shape dramatically changes as well.

We can create multiple plots with the same range along the *x*-axis using the code shown here:

```
#Import the required packages

from bokeh.io import output_file, show
from bokeh.layouts import row

#Creating equal x-axis ranges

plot2.x_range = plot1.x_range

#Create the row layout

row_layout = row(plot2, plot1)
```

```
#Output the plot

output_file('row.html')

show(row_layout)
```

This results in a row layout of plots as illustrated here:

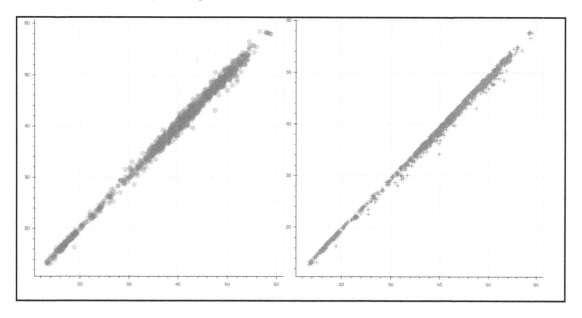

Plots 1 and 2 linked together using the same *x*-axis range as Plot 2

The most important point to note when linking multiple plots together is that the type of data in the *x*-/*y*-axis has to be the same. For instance, linking two plots along the *x*-axis in which one plot has a date (timestamp) type along the *x*-axis and the other plot has numbers will not work.

Summary

This chapter gave you an in-depth view of how you can use layouts in Bokeh to maximize the impact that your plots deliver—both statistically and visually.

You learned how to create plots in a horizontal layout, vertical layout, and a nested layout. You also learned how to use the grid layout as a more effective way to combine horizontal and vertical layouts together.

The standalone layout requires more lines of code to stack plots both horizontally and vertically in the same image, while the grid layout does this with a single line of code and is a more effective way to stack multiple plots together in different layout configurations.

Creating tabs in order to reduce clutter and linking multiple plots together to improve the comparative study of your data points are now in your tool belt in Bokeh.

In the next chapter, you will learn how to visually enhance the plots that you have created so far with annotations, widgets, and attributes that will add a world of interactivity to your plots!

5
Using Annotations, Widgets, and Visual Attributes for Visual Enhancement

Now that you have learned how to create plots and layouts in Bokeh, it is time to enhance them visually and add a layer of interactivity using annotations, widgets, and visual attributes.

Annotations are used to add supplemental information to your plots, such as titles, legends, and color maps that provide information about what the plot is trying to convey to the person who views your plot.

Widgets offer interactivity through buttons, drop-down menus, sliders, and textboxes. These widgets allow the person viewing the plot to interact with the plot and make changes to the way he or she wants to view it.

Visual attributes provide a vast range of visual enhancements to the plot, such as colors and fills for the lines and text, and interactivity enhancements such as the hover tool to hover over and select points of interest.

In this chapter, you will learn how to create:

- Annotations that convey supplemental information about your plots
- Widgets that add interactivity to your plots
- Visual attributes that enhance both the style and interactivity of your plots

Technical requirements

You will be required to have Python installed on a system. Finally, to use the Git repository of this book, the user needs to install Git.

The code files of this chapter can be found on GitHub:
`https://github.com/PacktPublishing/Hands-on-Data-Visualization-with-Bokeh.`

Check out the following video to see the code in action:

`http://bit.ly/2sYn4DN.`

Creating annotations to convey supplemental information

When creating plots it's fundamental to get across the story that the information in the plot is trying to convey. This can be done by adding titles, legends, and color maps to your plot.

Adding titles to plots

Titles are used to tell the reader about the overall story of the plot.

For the purposes of this chapter, we will use the **S&P 500 stock data** found on Kaggle. (`https://www.kaggle.com/camnugent/sandp500/data`).

We will also filter the data to just information about Apple stocks, as illustrated in the following code:

```
#Import the required packages

import pandas as pd

#Read in the data
```

```
df = pd.read_csv('all_stocks_5yr.csv')

#Convert the date column into datetime data type

df['date'] = pd.to_datetime(df['date'])

#Filter the data for Apple stocks only

df_apple = df[df['Name'] == 'AAL']
```

We will now store the required data in a `ColumnDataSource` object by using the code shown here:

```
#Import the required packages

from bokeh.io import output_file, show
from bokeh.plotting import figure
from bokeh.plotting import ColumnDataSource


#Create the ColumnDataSource object

data = ColumnDataSource(data = {
    'x' : df_apple['high'],
    'y' : df_apple['low'],
    'x1': df_apple['open'],
    'y1': df_apple['close'],
    'x2': df_apple['date'],
    'y2': df_apple['volume'],
})
```

In order to add a title to our plot, we use the code shown here:

```
#Import the required packages

from bokeh.plotting import figure, show, output_file, output_notebook

#Create the plot with the title

plot = figure(title = "5 year time series distribution of volume of Apple
stocks traded",title_location = "above",x_axis_type = 'datetime',
x_axis_label = 'date', y_axis_label = 'Volume Traded')

#Create the time series plot

plot.line(x = 'x2', y = 'y2', source = data, color = 'red')

plot.circle(x = 'x2', y = 'y2', source = data, fill_color = 'white', size =
```

```
3)

#Output the plot

output_file('title.html')

show(plot)
```

This results in a plot with a title, as illustrated here:

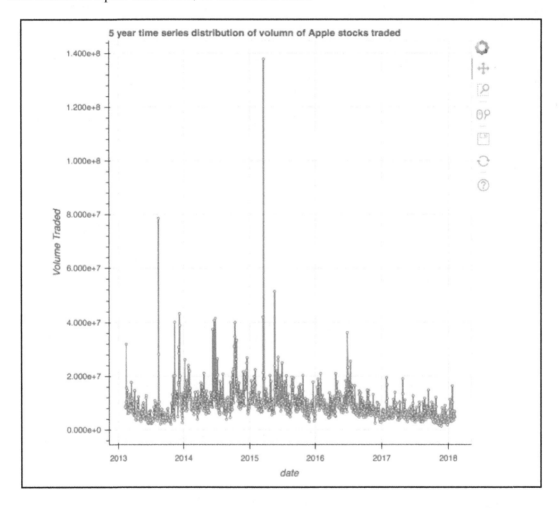

In this code, we used the `figure` function in order to generate the title by using the `title` argument. Additionally, we can also specify the location of the title using the `title_location` argument. The various locations for the title are `above`, `left`, `right`, and `below`.

Adding legends to plots

When we have a plot that has multiple colors for different visualizations in it, it is important for the reader to be able to distinguish between the different colors. This can be done by adding a legend to our plot.

In the following code, we plot two different scatter plots in the same plot, but with different colors. We add a legend to each scatter plot by using the code shown here:

```
#Import the required packages

from bokeh.plotting import figure, show, output_file

#Create the two scatter plots

plot = figure()

#Create the legends

plot.cross(x = 'x', y = 'y', source = data, color = 'red', size = 10, alpha
= 0.8, legend = "High Vs. Low")

plot.circle(x = 'x1', y = 'y1', source = data, color = 'green', size = 10,
alpha = 0.3, legend = "Open Vs. Close")

#Output the plot

output_file('legend.html')

show(plot)
```

This results in a plot with a legend, as illustrated here:

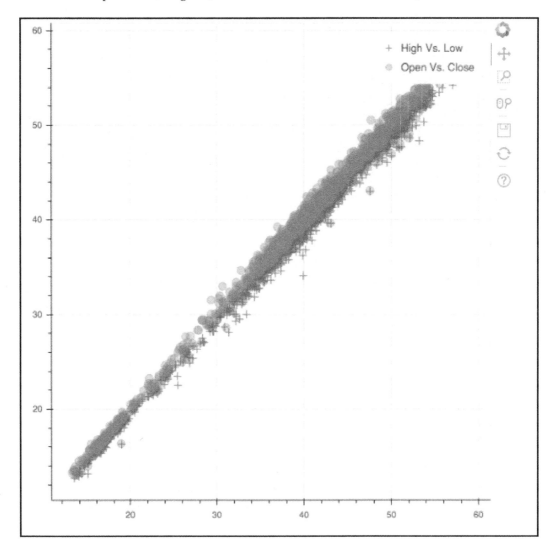

In this code, we used the `legend` argument while creating the individual scatter plots to specify the legend for that particular plot. We can now clearly distinguish what the green scatter plot and the red scatter plot mean thanks to the legend.

Adding color maps to plots

When we have categorical data, it is a good practice to color the different categories with different colors so that it becomes apparent to the reader that the different colors indicate different categories.

In order to do this, we first filter the S&P 500 stock data for two stocks: Google and USB using the code shown here:

```
#Reading in the S&P 500 data

df = pd.read_csv('all_stocks_5yr.csv')

#Filtering for Google or USB

df_multiple = df[(df['Name'] == 'GOOGL') | (df['Name'] == 'USB')]
```

Next, we are going to create a scatter plot between the high and low and categorically color the Google and USB stocks with different colors using the code shown here:

```
#Import the required packages

from bokeh.models import CategoricalColorMapper

#Store the data in the ColumnDataSource object

data = ColumnDataSource(df_multiple)

#Create the mapper

category_map = CategoricalColorMapper(
    factors = ['GOOGL', 'USB'], palette = ['blue', 'red'])

#Plot the figure

plot = figure()

plot.circle('high', 'low', size = 8, source = data, color = {'field':
'Name', 'transform': category_map})

#Output the plot

output_file('category.html')

show(plot)
```

This results in a plot as illustrated in the diagram:

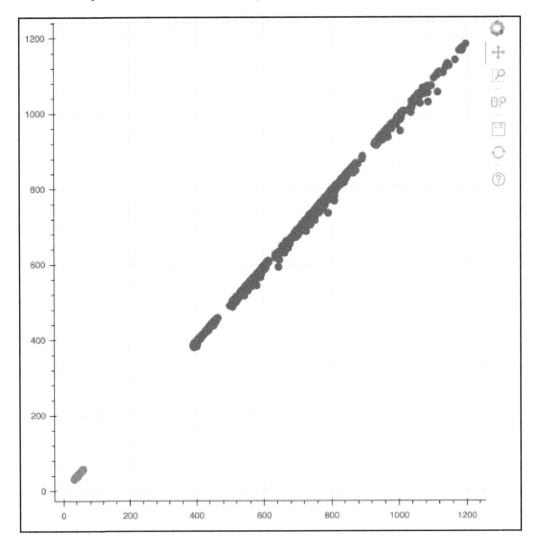

From the plot, it is evident that the two colors, blue and red, stand for the Google and USB stocks, respectively.

In this code, we used the `CategoricalColorMapper` function to assign a particular color to each stock. We then used the `color` argument while creating the plot to build a dictionary of the `field` or column that contains the categories and the category map that we created with the `CategoricalColorMapper`.

Creating widgets to add interactivity to plots

One of Bokeh's most unique features is the ability to add widgets that add interactivity to plots. Widgets allow the user of the plot to change what they want to see by making selections, clicking on buttons, and typing into textboxes. In this section, you will learn about all the widgets that Bokeh can add to your Toolbelt.

The two imports that you will need to create and output any kind of widget are given here:

```
from bokeh.io import output_file, show
from bokeh.layouts import widgetbox
```

Creating a button widget

Buttons allow a user to click and make a selection. We can create a button widget in Bokeh by using the code shown here:

```
#Import the required packages

from bokeh.models.widgets import Button

#Create the button widget

button_widget = Button(label="Click this")

#Output the button

output_file("button_widget.html")

show(widgetbox(button_widget))
```

This will create a button as illustrated in the diagram here:

In this code, we used the Button function to create a button that has the text **Click this.**

Creating the checkbox widget

Checkboxes allow users to make one or many selections. They are commonly used to select individual or multiple categories/plots when a plot has multiple categories and/or visualizations.

In order to create a simple checkbox in Bokeh, use the code shown here:

```
#Import the required packages

from bokeh.models.widgets import CheckboxGroup

#Create the checkbox

checkbox_widget = CheckboxGroup(
        labels=["box: 1", "box: 2", "box:3"], active=[1,2])

#Output the checkbox

output_file("checkbox_widget.html")

show(widgetbox(checkbox_widget))
```

This results in the creation of checkboxes as illustrated here:

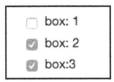

In this code, we have used the CheckboxGroup function to create three categories. The active argument is used to specify which of the three categories should remain checked when the checkbox is created. In this case, we configured active to check Boxes 2 and 3 upon creation.

Creating a drop-down menu widget

Drop-down menus can be used to choose from one of the many options available to the user. In order to build a drop-down menu, use the code shown here:

```
#Import the required packages

from bokeh.models.widgets import Dropdown
```

```
#Create the menu

menu_widget = [("menu option 1", "1"), ("menu option 2", "2")]

#Create the Dropdown

menu_dropdown = Dropdown(label="Dropdown Menu", menu=menu_widget)

#Output the dropdown menu

output_file("dropdown.html")

show(widgetbox(menu_dropdown))
```

This creates a **Dropdown Menu**, as illustrated here:

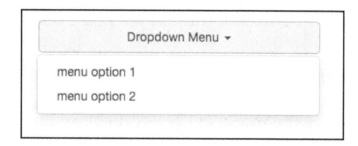

In this code, we first created a list of names that will appear in the menu of the drop-down. We then created the drop-down menu by using the `Dropdown` function and by passing the menu list into the `menu` argument.

Creating the radio button widget

Radio buttons limit the user's choice to pick just one option, instead of multiple options like the checkbox. Such buttons are useful when multiple selections result in an error. In order to construct a radio button, use the code shown here:

```
#Import the required packages

from bokeh.models.widgets import RadioGroup

#Create the radio button

radio_button_widget = RadioGroup(
        labels=["First Radio Button", "Second Radio Button"], active=0)
```

```
#Output the radio button widget

output_file("radiobutton_widget.html")

show(widgetbox(radio_button_widget))
```

This results in the creation of a radio button, as illustrated here:

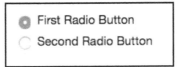

In this code, we used the `RadioGroup` function to create the radio buttons. The `labels` argument was used to specify the names of the buttons, while the `active` argument was used to specify which button was going to be selected by default.

Creating a slider widget

Sliders are used to increase or decrease a set number of points or a region that you might want to view in a plot. In order to construct a simple slider widget in Bokeh, use the code shown here:

```
#Import the required packages

from bokeh.models.widgets import Slider

#Create the slider widget

slider_widget = Slider(start=0, end=50, value=0, title="Simple Slider",
step = 5)

#Output the slider

output_file("slider_widget.html")

show(widgetbox(slider_widget))
```

This results in a slider widget, as illustrated in the figure here:

In this code, we used the `Slider` function in order to create the slider widget. The `start` argument was used to specify the starting value of the slider and the `end` argument was used to specify the last value that the slider would have, which in this case was *50*. The `value` argument was used to specify the value the slider would start at when it was generated. The `step` argument was used to specify the number of counts by which the slider's value would increase or decrease as it was moved to the right or left respectively. Finally, the `title` argument was used to give the slider a title.

Creating a text input widget

Text input boxes provide users with a way to type in text, which can be linked to changing the output of the plot, based on how you configured the plot beforehand. In order to create a text input widget, use the code shown here:

```
#Import the required packages

from bokeh.models.widgets import TextInput

#Create the text input widget

text_input_widget = TextInput(title="Type your text here", value = "")

#Output the text input widget

output_file("text_input_widget.html")

show(widgetbox(text_input_widget))
```

This results in a text input widget, as illustrated in the following screenshot:

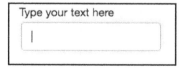

In this code, we used the `TextInput` function in order to create the text input widget. The `value` argument is used to set the default text that appears in the text input box upon creation of the text input widget. The `title` argument was used to specify the title of the text input widget and is important because the title usually gives the user of the plot directions on what he/she must type into the text input box.

Creating visual attributes to enhance style and interactivity

Visual attributes can broadly be classified into two categories:

- Attributes that add interactivity to your plot
- Attributes that enhance the visual style of your plot

This section will lay the foundation for both these categories and show how you can fully utilize and exploit Bokeh to get the most out of your plots.

Attributes that add interactivity to the plot

The visual attributes that further enhance the interactivity of your plots are as follows:

- **Hover Tooltip**: Lets you point the mouse at a specific point in the plot and displays associated information
- **Selection**: Lets you select a region of the plot and colors that region a different color

Creating a hover tooltip

In order to create a hover tooltip, we will use the code shown here:

```
#Import the required packages

from bokeh.models import CategoricalColorMapper
from bokeh.models import HoverTool
from bokeh.io import output_file, show
from bokeh.plotting import ColumnDataSource
from bokeh.plotting import figure
import pandas as pd
```

```
#Read in the data and filter for Google and USB stocks

df = pd.read_csv('all_stocks_5yr.csv')

df_multiple = df[(df['Name'] == 'GOOGL') | (df['Name'] == 'USB')]

#Create the hover tooltip

hover_tool = HoverTool(tooltips = [
    ('Stock Ticker', '@Name'),
    ('High Price', '@high'),
    ('Low Price', '@low')
])

#Save the data in a ColumnDataSource object

data = ColumnDataSource(df_multiple)

#Create the categorical color mapper

category_map = CategoricalColorMapper(
    factors = ['GOOGL', 'USB'], palette = ['blue', 'red'])

#Create the plot with the hover tooltip

plot = figure(tools = [hover_tool])

plot.circle('high', 'low', size = 8, source = data, color = {'field':
'Name', 'transform': category_map})

#Output the plot

output_file('hover.html')

show(plot)
```

This results in a plot with the hover tooltip displaying information about a particular point in the plot, as illustrated here:

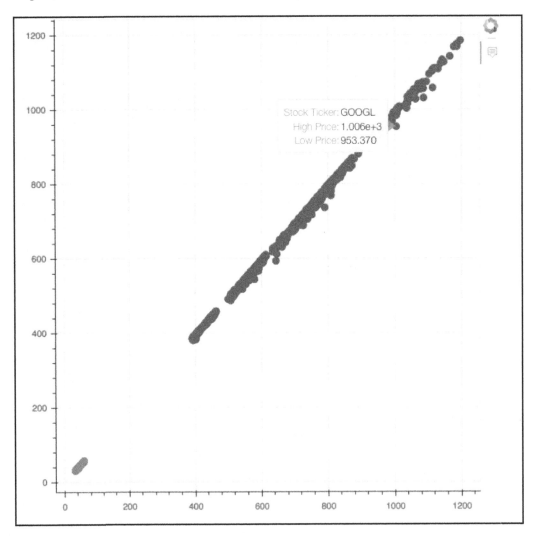

In this code, we reused the plot that we created for coloring different categories using the categorical color mapper. We used the `HoverTool` function to create a list of tuples. Each tuple contains the name of the information to be conveyed, such as `Stock Ticker`, and the associated column in which this information is found, such as `@Name`. We then passed this `HoverTool` object into the `tools` argument of the `figure` function while creating the plot.

Pointing the mouse at a particular point in the plot, we see information such as the stock ticker, high prices, and low prices displayed.

Creating selections

In order to select a region of the plot that we just created, we will use the code shown here:

```
#Import the required packages

from bokeh.models import CategoricalColorMapper
from bokeh.models import HoverTool
from bokeh.io import output_file, show
from bokeh.plotting import ColumnDataSource
from bokeh.plotting import figure

#Read in the dataset and filter for Google and USB stocks

df = pd.read_csv('all_stocks_5yr.csv')

df_multiple = df[(df['Name'] == 'GOOGL') | (df['Name'] == 'USB')]

#Save the data into a ColumnDataSource object

data = ColumnDataSource(df_multiple)

#Create the categorical color mapper

category_map = CategoricalColorMapper(
    factors = ['GOOGL', 'USB'], palette = ['blue', 'red'])

#Create the plot with the selection tool

plot = figure(tools = 'box_select')

plot.circle('high', 'low', size = 8, source = data,
            color = {'field': 'Name', 'transform': category_map},
selection_color = 'green',
            nonselection_fill_alpha = 0.3, nonselection_fill_color = 'grey')

#Output the plot

output_file('selection.html')

show(plot)
```

This results in the plot illustrated here:

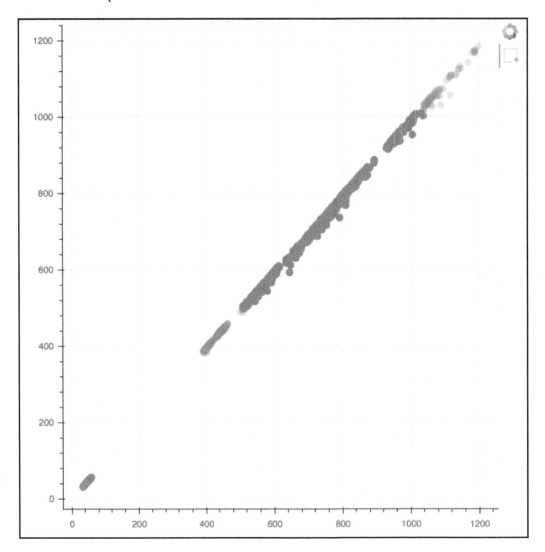

In this plot, the `Box Select` tool can be found in the top-right corner. Once we click the box select tool, we can drag and create a box on the plot to select a region of the plot. In the preceding plot, the selected regions appear in green while the regions that are not selected appear in gray.

In this code, we use the `selection_color` argument while creating the plot to specify the color that the plot will change to upon selection. We use `nonselection_fill_color` to specify the color that the unselected regions of the plot will take, which in this case is gray.

Finally, we use the `figure` function in order to specify the `tools`, which in this case is the `box_select` tool, which selects regions of the plot in squares.

Attributes that enhance the visual style of the plot

The attributes that enhance the visual style of the plot can be classified as follows:

- Styling the title
- Styling the background
- Styling the outline of the plot
- Styling the labels

Styling the title

Styling the title of the plot is a fantastic way to create a plot that's truly unique for the task at hand. In order to create a custom style for the plot, we use the code shown here:

```
#Import the required packages

from bokeh.models import CategoricalColorMapper
from bokeh.models import HoverTool
from bokeh.io import output_file, show
from bokeh.plotting import ColumnDataSource
from bokeh.plotting import figure

#Read in and filter the data for Google and USB stocks

df = pd.read_csv("all_stocks_5yr.csv")

df_multiple = df[(df['Name'] == 'GOOGL') | (df['Name'] == 'USB')]
```

```
#Store the data in a ColumnDataSource

data = ColumnDataSource(df_multiple)

#Create the categorical color mapper

category_map = CategoricalColorMapper(
    factors = ['GOOGL', 'USB'], palette = ['blue', 'red'])

#Create the plot and configure the title

plot = figure(title = "High Vs. Low Prices (Google & USB)")

plot.title.text_color = "red"

plot.title.text_font = "times"

plot.title.text_font_style = "bold"

plot.circle('high', 'low', size = 8, source = data,
            color = {'field': 'Name', 'transform': category_map})

#Output the plot

output_file('title.html')

show(plot)
```

This results in a plot with a unique title, as illustrated here:

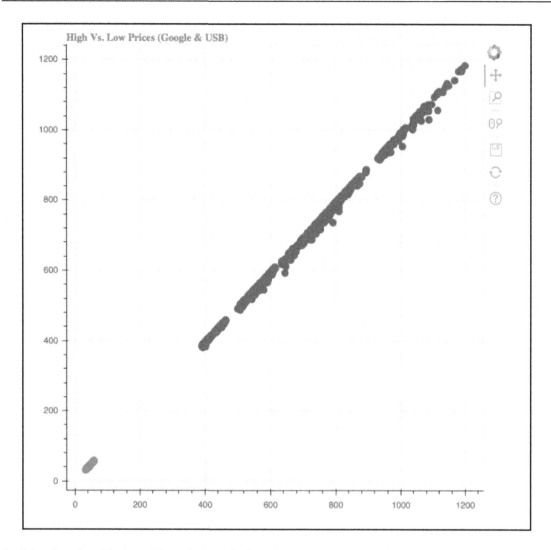

In this plot, the title is red in color, with the Times New Roman font, and is bold. In this code, we used `title.text_color` to give the title a red color. We then used `title.text_font` to give the title the Times New Roman font. Finally, we used `title.text_font_style` to give the plot a bold font.

Styling the background

The background of your plot can be styled to give it different colors. This is particularly useful when we want the points in our plot to stand out against a contrasting background. We can customize and style the background of our plot by using the code shown here:

```
#Import the required packages

from bokeh.models import CategoricalColorMapper
from bokeh.models import HoverTool
from bokeh.io import output_file, show
from bokeh.plotting import ColumnDataSource
from bokeh.plotting import figure

#Read in the data and filter for Google and USB stocks

df = pd.read_csv("all_stocks_5yr.csv")

df_multiple = df[(df['Name'] == 'GOOGL') | (df['Name'] == 'USB')]

#Save the data in a ColumnDataSource object

data = ColumnDataSource(df_multiple)

#Create the categorical color mapper

category_map = CategoricalColorMapper(
    factors = ['GOOGL', 'USB'], palette = ['blue', 'red'])

#Create the plot and configure the background

plot = figure(title = "High Vs. Low Prices (Google & USB)")

plot.background_fill_color = "yellow"
plot.background_fill_alpha = 0.3

plot.circle('high', 'low', size = 8, source = data,
            color = {'field': 'Name', 'transform': category_map})

#Output the plot

output_file('title.html')

show(plot)
```

This results in a plot with a yellow background, as illustrated here:

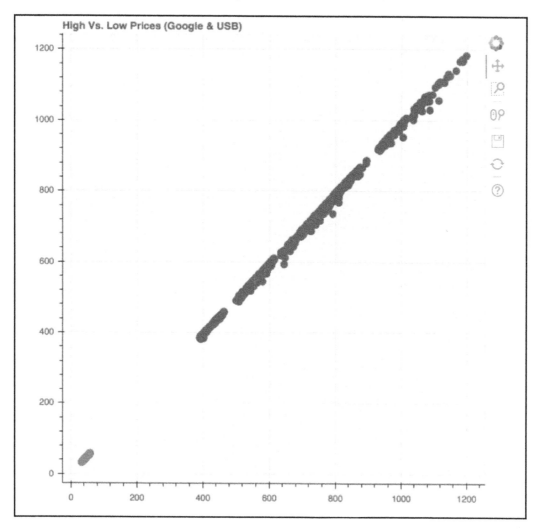

We can now see that the plot has been enhanced and that the red and blue points stand out more prominently thanks to the yellow background.

In this code, we used `background_fill_color` to give the plot the yellow background. We then used `background_fill_alpha` to give our background a little transparency.

Styling the outline of the plot

Styling the outline of our plot is a wonderful way to give the plot a strong and well-defined border that enhances the overall aesthetic of the plot, giving it a portrait effect. This can be done using the code shown here:

```
#Import the required packages

from bokeh.models import CategoricalColorMapper
from bokeh.models import HoverTool
from bokeh.io import output_file, show
from bokeh.plotting import ColumnDataSource
from bokeh.plotting import figure

#Read in the data and filter for Google and USB stocks

df = pd.read_csv("all_stocks_5yr.csv")

df_multiple = df[(df['Name'] == 'GOOGL') | (df['Name'] == 'USB')]

#Save data into a ColumnDataSource object

data = ColumnDataSource(df_multiple)

#Create the color mapper

category_map = CategoricalColorMapper(
    factors = ['GOOGL', 'USB'], palette = ['blue', 'red'])

plot = figure(title = "High Vs. Low Prices (Google & USB)")

#Configure the outline of the plot

plot.outline_line_width = 8
plot.outline_line_alpha = 0.8
plot.outline_line_color = "black"

#Create and output the plot

plot.circle('high', 'low', size = 8, source = data,
            color = {'field': 'Name', 'transform': category_map})

output_file('outline.html')

show(plot)
```

This results in a plot with a black outline, as illustrated in the image here:

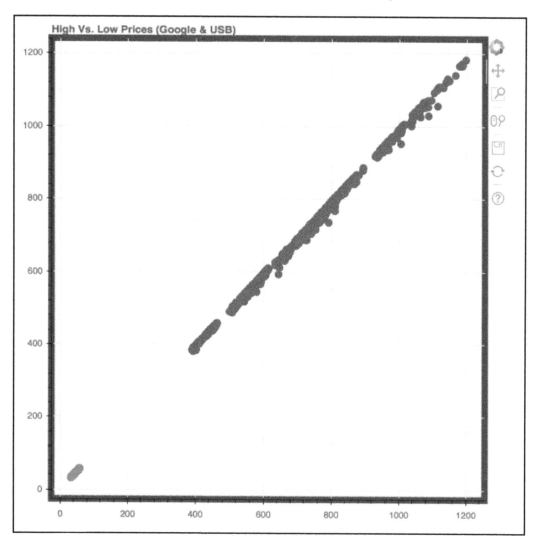

In this code, we used `outline_line_width` to configure the width of our outline. A higher value would result in a broader outline. We then used `outline_line_alpha` to configure the transparency of the outline. A higher value would result in a less transparent outline. Finally, we used `outline_line_color` to give the outline a black color.

Styling the labels

Giving the labels of your plot a unique font and color gives you a higher level of customizability for your plot. In order to customize the labels of our plot, we will use the code shown here:

```
#Import the required packages

from bokeh.models import CategoricalColorMapper
from bokeh.models import HoverTool
from bokeh.io import output_file, show
from bokeh.plotting import ColumnDataSource
from bokeh.plotting import figure

#Read in the data

df = pd.read_csv("all_stocks_5yr.csv")

df_multiple = df[(df['Name'] == 'GOOGL') | (df['Name'] == 'USB')]

#Save the data as a ColumnDataSource object

data = ColumnDataSource(df_multiple)

#Create a categorical color mapper

category_map = CategoricalColorMapper(
    factors = ['GOOGL', 'USB'], palette = ['blue', 'red'])

#Create the plot and configure the labels

plot = figure(title = "High Vs. Low Prices (Google & USB)")

plot.xaxis.axis_label = "High Prices"
plot.xaxis.axis_label_text_color = "green"

plot.yaxis.axis_label = "Low Prices"
plot.yaxis.axis_label_text_font_style = "bold"

plot.circle('high', 'low', size = 8, source = data,
            color = {'field': 'Name', 'transform': category_map})

#Output the plot

output_file('title.html')

show(plot)
```

This results in a plot with customized labels, as illustrated here:

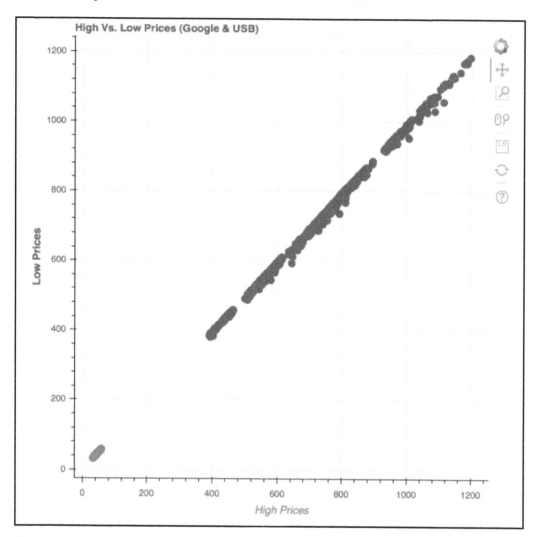

In this plot, we can observe that the *x*-axis label is green in color, while the *y*-axis label is bold. In this code, we used `axis_label_text_color` to give the label a unique color of our choice and `axis_label_text_font_style` to give the label a bold font style.

Summary

This chapter has shed light on all the different tools that you can utilize to add layers of interactivity and visually appealing aesthetics to your plots.

You have learned how to use annotations to add titles, legends, and categorical color maps to your plots in order to convey supplemental information about the plot. You also learned how to build all the different types of widget that Bokeh offers in order to make your plots more interactive. Finally, you also learned about visual attributes that add both interactivity and style to your visualizations.

In the next chapter, you will learn how to combine everything you have learned in this chapter and the previous chapters into an interactive application that will enthrall both yourself and the users of your plots!

6
Building and Hosting Applications Using the Bokeh Server

Bokeh gives its users the flexibility and convenience of hosting real-time applications on its own servers. The Bokeh Server serves as a bridge connecting Python and the browser in which you can host your applications. In fact, you have been using the Bokeh Server all this time while you were creating your plots in a Jupyter Notebook by following the code in the chapters before this!

One of the ways you can use the Bokeh Server is to deploy applications that have interactivity locally on your machine, which you can then share with your colleagues.

In this chapter, you will be given an:

- Introduction to the Bokeh Server
- Introduction to building a Bokeh application
- Introduction to deploying the Bokeh application

This chapter aims to build your fundamentals with respect to the Bokeh Server so that we can build a beautiful and interactive real-time Bokeh application in the last chapter of the book!

Technical requirements

You will be required to have Python installed on a system. Finally, to use the Git repository of this book, the user needs to install Git.

The code files of this chapter can be found on GitHub:
`https://github.com/PacktPublishing/Hands-on-Data-Visualization-with-Bokeh`.

Check out the following video to see the code in action:

`http://bit.ly/2LGCqEC`.

Introduction to the Bokeh Server

Before creating our very own application using the Bokeh Server, it is important to formulate a clear picture of what the Bokeh Server actually is.

In very simple terms, the Bokeh objects that you create, such as the plots, axes, widgets, and almost anything and everything to do with your interactive visualization, are coded by you in Python. These Bokeh objects are then converted to JSON format by Bokeh.

In order to visualize this process, have a look at this diagram:

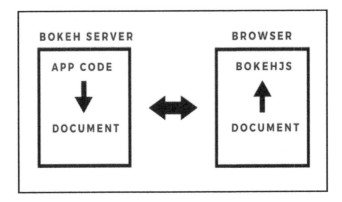

Within the context of the **BOKEH SERVER**, the Python code that you write is going to be converted to a **JSON DOCUMENT**. The **JSON DOCUMENT** is then rendered in JavaScript by the client library called **BOKEHJS** so that we can view the application in our **BROWSER**.

Bokeh does all of this for you, so no prior knowledge of JavaScript is required to make an application!

Building a Bokeh application

Every Bokeh application has a structure to it. This structure helps break the large application down into smaller components that can be built individually and then put back together to render the application as a whole. This structure is illustrated here:

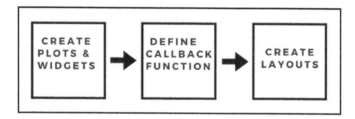

As depicted in the diagram, the first step to building an end-to-end application in Bokeh is to create the plots and widgets that you would like to see in your application. **CREATING PLOTS & WIDGETS** is a concept that you should be comfortable with at this stage.

The next step is to **DEFINE CALLBACK FUNCTION**. The callback function is simply a function that tells the application how to respond when a user interacts with your application. For example, if you create a button called Update Plot, the function will update the plot with new data that it retrieves from the web. In other words, the callback function serves as a bridge that connects the widgets that you create and how these widgets interact and make changes to your plot.

The final step is **CREATE LAYOUTS** in order to present your plots in the most effective and aesthetically pleasing way possible. Once again, creating and customizing layouts is a concept you are now familiar with at this point in time.

Combining these three steps will render your very own Bokeh application!

Creating a single slider application

In the previous chapter, you learned how to create a simple slider widget in your Jupyter Notebook. However, that widget was not an application that could be used by you or by the people in your internal team/wider audience.

For the purpose of creating applications, we will use a text editor instead of a Jupyter Notebook. You can use any text editor of your choice. Once you copy and paste the code shown next into your text editor, you have to ensure that you save the file as bokeh.py or any {name}.py, as long as it has a .py extension to it.

In your terminal (for the MacOS/Linux) or PowerShell (Windows), you will need to go to the directory in which you have saved the file in order to launch the application.

In order to create a simple single slider application in Bokeh, we use the code shown here:

```
#Import the required packages

from bokeh.layouts import widgetbox
from bokeh.models import Slider
from bokeh.io import curdoc

#Create a slider widget

slider_widget = Slider(start = 0, end = 100, step = 10, title = 'Single
Slider')

#Create a layout for the widget

slider_layout = widgetbox(slider_widget)

#Add the slider widget to the application

curdoc().add_root(slider_layout)
```

In this code, we created a simple single slider widget that starts at 0 and ends at 100. We then added this slider into a layout using the widgetbox function. Finally, we used the curdoc function in order to embed the slider widget into our application by calling the add_root method.

Whenever we create an application, Bokeh creates a blank document or canvas for that application. This blank document is known as curdoc. We can add widgets, plots, and elements of interest to this blank document by using the add_root method.

The difference this time around is that we do not type the preceding code into a Jupyter Notebook cell and execute it. Instead, we save the preceding code using a text editor. You will have to ensure that the preceding code is given a .py extension. For example, the preceding code was saved as bokeh.py using a text editor.

In order to run the application, you will open up the terminal if you are on Mac/Linux, or the Windows Shell if you are on a Windows machine, and type the command shown here:

```
bokeh serve --show bokeh.py
```

This will launch your Bokeh application in your browser, as illustrated here:

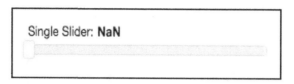

Although we configured the slider widget to start at 0 and end at 100, it will not display this because the slider widget is not linked to any data source that it can work on. This is why we define a callback function to connect your plots and widgets together via a data source, as explained in the *Introduction to the Bokeh Server* Section.

Creating a multi-slider application

In this section, we are going to create an application with three sliders. To do this, we use the code shown here:

```
#Import the required packages

from bokeh.layouts import widgetbox
from bokeh.models import Slider
from bokeh.io import curdoc

#Create multiple slider widgets

slider_widget1 = Slider(start = 0, end = 100, step = 10, title = 'Slider
1')

slider_widget2 = Slider(start = 0, end = 50, step = 5, title = 'Slider 2')

slider_widget3 = Slider(start = 50, end = 100, step = 5, title = 'Slider
3')
```

```
#Create a layout for the widget

slider_layout = widgetbox(slider_widget1, slider_widget2, slider_widget3)

#Add the slider widget to the application

curdoc().add_root(slider_layout)
```

In the preceding code, we created three slider widgets and then added them in the
widgetbox function. We then executed the application using the Terminal/Shell, as shown
here:

```
bokeh serve --show bokeh.py
```

This results in the application shown here:

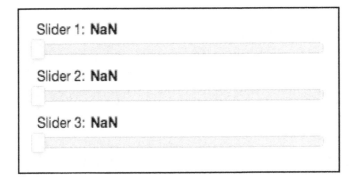

We now have an application that makes use of three sliders instead of one.

Combining the slider application with a scatter plot

The fundamental purpose of the slider application is fulfilled only when we can use it to
add a layer of interactivity to our plots. We can combine a simple scatter plot with a slider
and host this as an application using the code shown here:

```
#Import the required packages

from bokeh.models import Slider, ColumnDataSource
from bokeh.io import curdoc
from bokeh.layouts import row
from bokeh.plotting import figure
```

```
from numpy.random import random

#Create data for the plot

initial_points = 500

data_points = ColumnDataSource(data = {'x': random(initial_points), 'y':
random(initial_points)})

#Create the plot

plot = figure(title = "Random scatter plot generator")

plot.diamond(x = 'x', y = 'y', source = data_points, color = 'red')

#Create the slider widget

slider_widget = Slider(start = 0, end = 10000, step = 10, value =
initial_points, title = 'Slide right to increase number of points')

#Define the callback function

def callback(attr, old, new):
    points = slider_widget.value
    data_points.data = {'x': random(points), 'y': random(points)}
slider_widget.on_change('value', callback)

#Create a layout for the application

layout = row(slider_widget, plot)

#Add the layout to the application

curdoc().add_root(layout)
```

We can now execute this script by using the command shown here:

```
bokeh serve --show bokeh.py
```

This results in the application shown here:

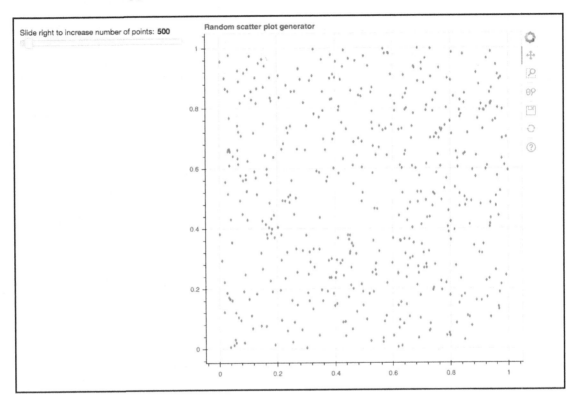

In the preceding code, we first defined an initial number of points that we wanted displayed in our scatter plot. This number is 500.

We then used the `ColumnDataSource` in order to define the data for the x and y variables by using the random function from `NumPy`. Fundamentally, x and y generate a random set of 500 numbers each, and this is used to generate the scatter plot displayed previously.

Next, we created a slider function that starts at 0 data points and ends at 10,000 points, with the initial value of the slider at the initial number of data points that we defined earlier, which is 500.

The most important part that makes the slider work for us is the `callback` function. Inside this function, we defined a variable called `points`, which essentially takes the possible values that the slider can take, which in this case is any value between 0 and 10,000.

We then defined the data that the slider will change when we move the slider from left to right or vice versa by using the `data_points.data` variable.

Finally we used the `on_change` method on the slider widget essentially to tell the slider that it has to change the `values` of the data as we move the slider in either direction.

As a result, this diagram shows us what happens when the slider is at 70 points and when the slider is at 9030 points:

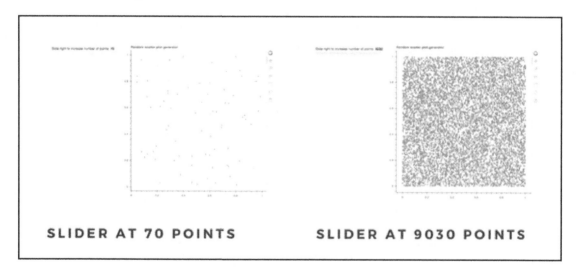

SLIDER AT 70 POINTS   **SLIDER AT 9030 POINTS**

We can clearly observe how the number of points seen on the scatter plot drastically increases with the addition of more points using the slider.

Such an application can be used when we want to have complete control over how much of the data we want to see, as sometimes fewer or more data points might reveal interesting insights.

Combining the slider application with a line plot

In this section, we will see how we can extend the functionalities of a slider application in the use case of a line plot. In order to construct a slider application with a line plot, we use the code shown here:

```
#Import the required packages

from bokeh.models import Slider, ColumnDataSource
from bokeh.io import curdoc
from bokeh.layouts import row
from bokeh.plotting import figure
from numpy.random import random

#Define the points that create the line plot

x = [1,2,3,4,5,6,7,8,9]
y = [2,3,4,5,6,7,8,9,10]

#Create the data source

data_points = ColumnDataSource(data = {'x': x, 'y': y})

#Create the line plot

plot = figure(title = 'Random Line plot generator')

plot.line('x', 'y', source = data_points, color = 'red')

#Create the slider widget

slider_widget = Slider(start = 0, end = 100, step = 1, value = 10)

#Define the callback function

def callback(attr, old, new):
    points = slider_widget.value
    data_points.data = {'x': random(points), 'y': random(points)}
slider_widget.on_change('value', callback)

#Create the layout

layout = row(slider_widget, plot)

#Add the layout to the application

curdoc().add_root(layout)
```

We can now execute this script by using the code shown here in the Terminal/Shell:

```
bokeh serve --show bokeh.py
```

This results in the application shown here:

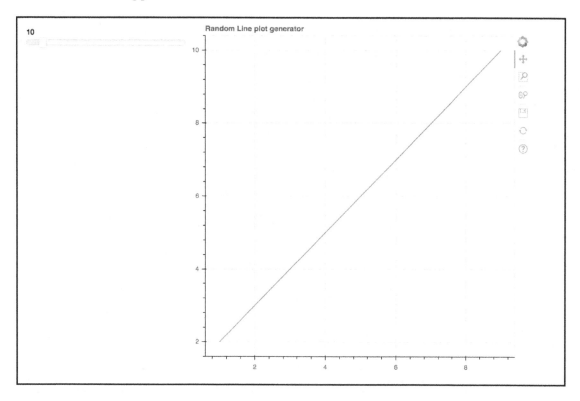

In the preceding code, we created a simple line plot and added a slider widget that can increase in value from 0 to 100.

We then defined a callback function, which takes the value of the slider as the `points` variable. Thus, the `points` variable can store any value from 0 to 100.

Next, we defined the data that the slider has to update every time we move the slider. In the preceding code, we gave the variables x and y random values from the `points` variable, as our aim was to create a random line plot generator.

Finally, we created a layout with the slider widget and the plot, and added this layout to the application.

On initial launch of the application, we can see that the application displays a straight line as this was the initial plot that was created by us. If we moved the slider to have 48 points, we would get a line plot that is generated randomly with 48 points for both the x and y variables, as illustrated here:

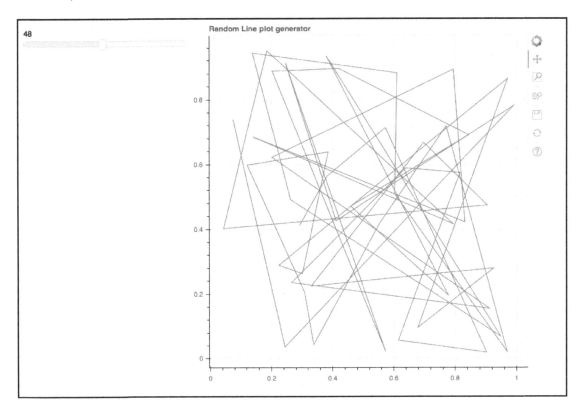

Thus, we see how the slider application can be used with the line plot in order to generate new plots with a different number of points.

Creating an application with the select widget

In this section, we are going to create an application that is used to change the distribution of the data. We will give our user two options to select from: a uniform distribution and a normal distribution. We can do this by using the code shown here:

```
#Import the required packages

from bokeh.models import Select, ColumnDataSource
```

```
from bokeh.io import curdoc
from bokeh.layouts import row
from bokeh.plotting import figure
from numpy.random import random, normal

#Create data for the plot

initial_points = 500

data_points = ColumnDataSource(data = {'x': random(initial_points), 'y':
random(initial_points)})

#Create the plot

plot = figure(title = "Scatter plot distribution selector")

plot.diamond(x = 'x', y = 'y', source = data_points, color = 'red')

#Create the select widget

select_widget = Select(options = ['uniform distribution', 'normal
distribution'], value = 'uniform distribution', title = 'Select the
distribution of your choice')

#Define the callback function

def callback(attr, old, new):
    if select_widget.value == 'uniform distribution':
        function = random
    else:
        function = normal
    data_points.data = {'x': function(size = initial_points), 'y':
function(size = initial_points)}

select_widget.on_change('value', callback)

#Create a layout for the application

layout = row(select_widget, plot)

#Add the layout to the application

curdoc().add_root(layout)
```

We can now run the application by using the code shown here:

```
bokeh serve --show bokeh.py
```

This results in the application shown here:

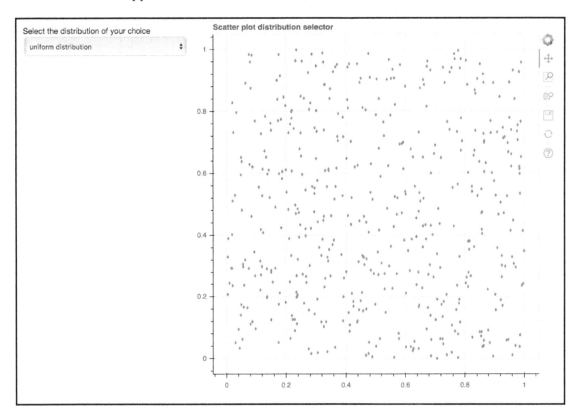

In the preceding code that we used to create this application, we created a random scatter plot with 500 points. We then created a select widget that has two options: a uniform distribution and a normal distribution.

In the callback function that we defined, if the user selects a uniform distribution, the function is set to `random` and if the user selects a normal distribution, the function is set to `normal`. These functions are then applied to the data points based on the selection that the user has made in your application.

In the previous screenshot, we applied the random function to the data points in order to create a uniform distribution and this was set as the default distribution that the application displays upon launch.

However, if we changed the distribution to that of a normal distribution, we would obtain a scatter plot as illustrated here:

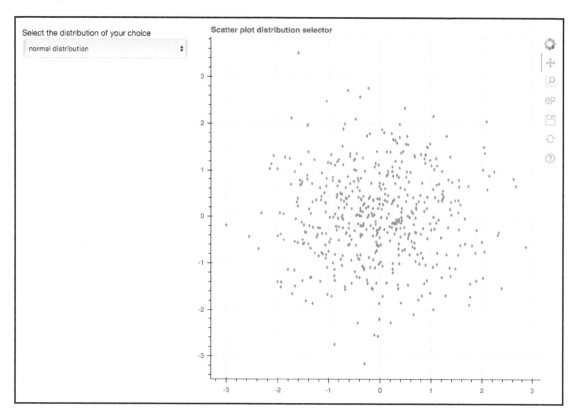

We can now observe how the scatter plot changes when we change the distribution of the points. Such applications are useful to look at our data from different perspectives, using different distributions, in order to capture insights that we normally could not have captured before.

Creating an application with the button widget

In this section, we are going to create an application with a button widget that will change how the data is displayed when you click it. In order to create such an application, we use the code shown here:

```
#Import the required packages

from bokeh.models import Button, ColumnDataSource
from bokeh.io import curdoc
from bokeh.layouts import row
from bokeh.plotting import figure
from numpy.random import random, normal
import numpy as np

#Create data for the plot

initial_points = 500

data_points = ColumnDataSource(data = {'x': random(initial_points), 'y':
random(initial_points)})

#Create the plot

plot = figure(title = "Data change application")

plot.diamond(x = 'x', y = 'y', source = data_points, color = 'red')

#Create the button widget

button_widget = Button(label = 'Change Data')

#Define the callback function

def callback():
    #New y values
    y = np.cos(initial_points) + random(initial_points)
    data_points.data = {'x': random(initial_points), 'y': y}
button_widget.on_click(callback)

#Create a layout for the application

layout = row(button_widget, plot)

#Add the layout to the application

curdoc().add_root(layout)
```

Using this script, we can execute the application using the command shown here:

```
bokeh serve --show bokeh.py
```

This results in the launch of the application shown here:

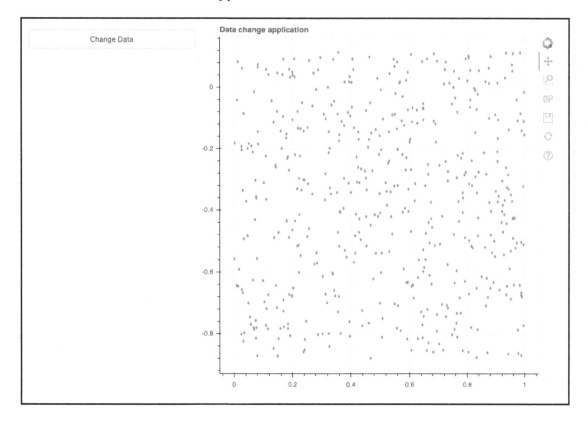

In the preceding code, we first created a random scatter plot with 500 points. We then created a button widget and defined the `callback` function.

Within the construct of the callback function, we give the points along the *y*-axis new values by using the `cos` and `random` functions of NumPy.

We then fed the values of *y* into the `ColumnDataSource`. Every time we click the button, the scatter plot updates itself with the new values of *y* that we have specified. This is shown here:

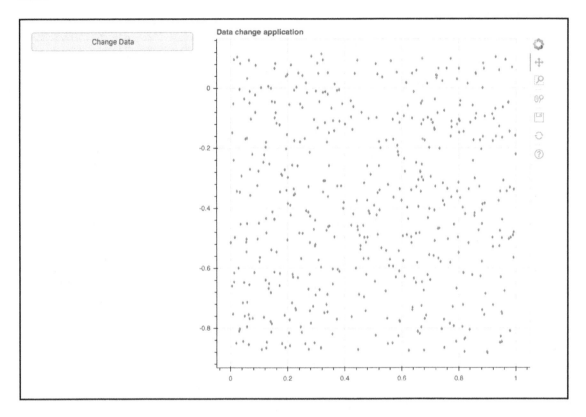

Although not significantly different, the points have changed location from the first plot. Thus, you can see how you can use the button function to update your plots and allow the user to see different versions of a single plot by modifying how the data is manipulated.

Creating an application to select different columns

A small example of using Bokeh in order to create an application in which you, as the user, can select different columns to be displayed on the *x*- and *y*-axes is illustrated in the code shown here:

```
#Importing the required packages

import pandas as pd
from bokeh.plotting import figure
from bokeh.models import ColumnDataSource, Select
from bokeh.io import curdoc
from bokeh.layouts import row

#Read in the data

df = pd.read_csv('all_stocks_5yr.csv')

#Filtering for apple stocks

df_apple = df[df['Name'] == 'AAL']

#Create the ColumnDataSource object

data = ColumnDataSource(data = {
    'x' : df_apple['high'],
    'y' : df_apple['low'],
    'x1': df_apple['volume']
})

#Creating the scatter plot

plot = figure(title = 'Attribute selector application')

plot.diamond('x', 'y', source = data, color = 'red')

#Creating the select widget

select_widget = Select(options = ['low', 'volume'], value = 'low', title =
'Select a new y axis attribute')

#Define the callback function

def callback(attr, old, new):
    if new == 'low':
```

```
        data.data = {'x' : df_apple['high'], 'y': df_apple['low']}
    else:
        data.data = {'x' : df_apple['high'], 'y': df_apple['volume']}
select_widget.on_change('value', callback)


#Add the layout to the application

layout = row(select_widget, plot)

curdoc().add_root(layout)
```

We can then launch this application by using the command shown here:

```
bokeh serve --show bokeh.py
```

This results in the application shown here:

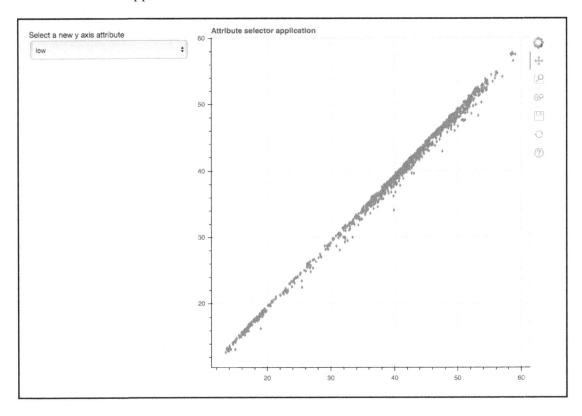

In the preceding code, we first loaded in the 5-year stock data, which can be found on Kaggle here: `https://www.kaggle.com/camnugent/sandp500/data`.

We then filtered the data to include Apple stocks only and added the attributes/columns of interest within the construct of the `ColumnDataSource`.

Next, we created a select widget with two options, `low` and `volume`, and we set the default option to `low`.

We constructed the callback function in such a way that if the user selects the `low` option, the application will display a scatter plot between the `high` and `low` values of the Apple stock, and if the user selects the `volume` option, the application will display a scatter plot between `high` and `volume`.

Selecting the `volume` option results in the scatter plot shown here:

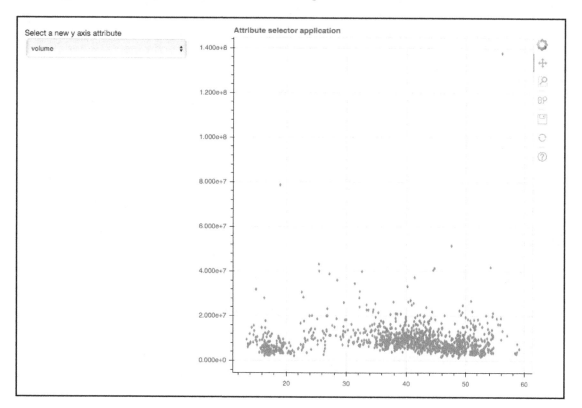

Thus, we see how an application like this can be used to display multiple plots within a single browser tab, and as such can be used to present a wide array of information to your users.

Introduction to deploying the Bokeh application

In the previous sections, we deployed our Bokeh applications using our local machine, which could then be shared with our colleagues in our internal team.

In order to deploy a Bokeh application, we first wrote a script in Python that included the the plot, the callback function, and the layout. We then gave the script an appropriate name. In the previous example, we gave our scripts the name `bokeh.py`.

Using the Terminal for Mac/Linux or the shell for Windows, we deployed the application from the directory in which the Python script was located with the command shown here:

```
bokeh serve --show bokeh.py
```

This launches the application in the default browser of your choice as:

```
http://localhost:5006/bokeh
```

In this case, we were making use of the Bokeh Server in order to run and deploy our application.

Summary

This chapter has given you the fundamentals when it comes to building and deploying your very own *Bokeh* applications on your local machine.

You have learned how to construct basic applications using the select widget, slider widget, and button widget, and how such applications can be used for a variety of applications.

In the future chapter, you will learn how to build your very own application using real-time data in order to create a statistically significant and aesthetically pleasing application.

7

Advanced Plotting with Networks, Geo Data, WebGL, and Exporting Plots

Adding interactivity to plots that are used to visualize networks such as social networks and transport networks allows the user to highlight and interact with the specific parts that they are interested in, while ignoring the rest of the network. This is particularly useful when you have a large and complex network.

Interactivity in geographic data is particularly useful when it comes to extracting information about a specific location of interest, instead of looking at the entire plot. Such geo-based visualizations help us zoom into locations and embed these maps into our applications.

When working with large and complex datasets, it is in our best interests to exploit the performance of Bokeh fully in terms of speed. We can do this with WebGL.

Finally, there are certain cases in which we might want to publish the plots that we create with Bokeh in books and journals with a high level of image quality. We can export our plots in PNG format by using Bokeh's export capabilities.

In this chapter, you will learn about:

- Using Bokeh to visualize networks
- Using Bokeh to visualize geographic data
- Using WebGL to improve performance
- Using Bokeh to export plots as PNG images

Technical requirements

You will be required to have Python installed on a system. Finally, to use the Git repository of this book, the user needs to install Git.

The code files of this chapter can be found on GitHub:
`https://github.com/PacktPublishing/Hands-on-Data-Visualization-with-Bokeh`.

Check out the following video to see the code in action:

`http://bit.ly/2HCCUJJ`.

Using Bokeh to visualize networks

Networks help you visualize relationships between people and items. For example, a simple network can show you how people are related to each other. This is illustrated for you in the following diagram:

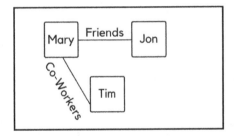

In this network, it is easy to see that Mary and Jon are friends, while Mary and Tim are coworkers. We can also see that Tim and Jon have no relationship at all. Such networks have powerful applications, especially in the field of social networks!

In this section, we are going to learn how to construct an interactive network using Bokeh. On a fundamental level, there are two ways to do this. The first is to construct and visualize these networks using the default straight lines to connect two nodes together, and the next is to construct and visualize these networks by defining a shape for the path that we choose.

Visualizing networks with straight paths

The first step is to import the required packages:

```
import math
from bokeh.io import show, output_file
from bokeh.plotting import figure
from bokeh.models import GraphRenderer, StaticLayoutProvider, Oval
from bokeh.palettes import Spectral10
```

The packages that are new here are `math`, `GraphRenderer`, `StaticLayoutProvider`, `Oval`, and `Spectral10`. As we progress into building our very own network, you will see why and when the following packages are used.

In this example, we are going to build a network with 10 nodes. Let's construct a list from 0 to 9, which we can use as the points of the nodes in our network. This is illustrated for you in the code shown here:

```
total_nodes = 10
node_points = list(range(total_nodes))
print(node_points)
```

As a result of the preceding code, we have 10 node points that we will incorporate into our network from 0 to 9:

```
#Output of print(node_points)

[0, 1, 2, 3, 4, 5, 6, 7, 8, 9]
```

The next step is to construct the plot that is going to our network and render it as a network graph. We can do this by using the code shown here:

```
plot = figure(x_range=(-1.1,1.1), y_range=(-1.1,1.1))

network = GraphRenderer()
```

In the preceding code, we created a figure by specifying the x and y ranges. In the preceding example, our range is -1.1 to $+1.1$. This gives us a considerably visible network. Increasing the size of the x and y ranges to, say, -10 to + 10 would render a smaller network.

Finally, the `GraphRenderer` function is used to create and render the network of interest.

The next step is to customize your network. We can do this by using the code shown here:

```
network.node_renderer.data_source.add(Spectral10, 'color')
```

In the preceding code, we are giving each node of our network one of the 10 unique colors from the Spectral10 package. This is illustrated here:

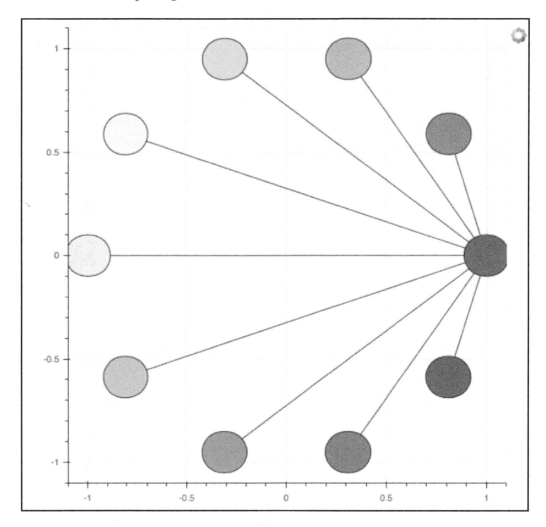

If we want all our nodes to have the same color, we can completely skip writing the preceding code.

In order to add the node points to the network, we use the code shown here:

```
network.node_renderer.data_source.add(node_points, 'index')
```

In order to customize the shape, size, and color of the network, we use the code shown here:

```
network.node_renderer.glyph = Oval(height=0.2, width=0.3,
fill_color='color')
```

If we wanted to create a network with bigger nodes, where each node was red, we would modify the code shown before to this:

```
network.node_renderer.glyph = Oval(height=0.4, width=0.5, fill_color='red')
```

This renders the network shown here:

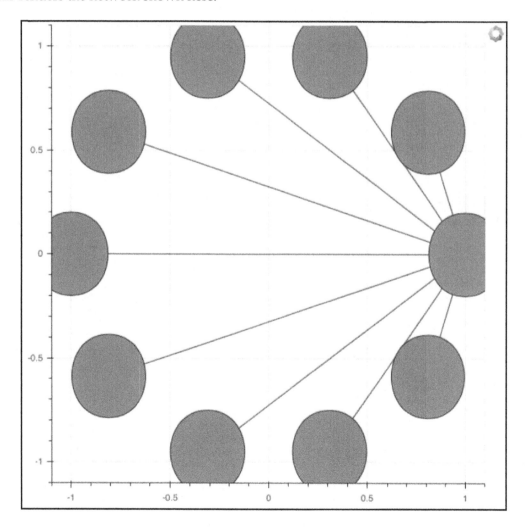

The next step is to configure the edge connections in the network. An edge is simply a link that connects two nodes together. To do this, we use the code shown here:

```
network.edge_renderer.data_source.data = dict(start=[1]*total_nodes,
end=node_points)
```

To create an edge, we simply create a dictionary that maps sets of points to each other. In the preceding code, the `start` argument is equal to the list containing the number 1 multiplied by the total number of nodes, which is 10. This results in the list shown here:

```
#Output of [1] * total_nodes:

[10,10,10,10,10,10,10,10,10,10]
```

The argument end contains `node_points`, which is a list that we defined earlier that goes from 0 to 9:

```
#Output of total_nodes:

[0,1,2,3,4,5,6,7,8,9]
```

In other words, we are mapping the two lists together:

```
{10:0, 10:1, 10:2, 10:3, 10:4, 10:5, 10:6, 10:7, 10:8, 10:9}
```

This results in node 10 being mapped to every other node in the network. This is illustrated in the output shown here:

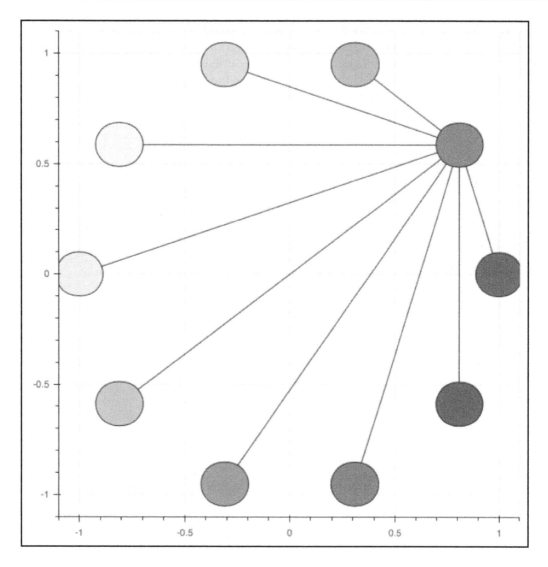

Fundamentally, the code that we created so far is enough to design your network, but is not sufficient to render the output of the network in your browser / Jupyter Notebook.

We need to use the layout provider model in order to render this network in two-dimensional space. In order to render an object in two-dimensional space, we need to specify the x and y coordinates of each node in two-dimensional space. We do this by extracting the circumference of each node and then using the cosine function along with the circumference to build the x and y coordinates for each node.

The first step is to create a list of circumferences for each node. We can do this by using the code shown here:

```
#Extracting the circumference of each node

node_circumference = [node*2*math.pi/10 for node in node_points]
```

If you recall, `node_points` is a list of points for each node ranging from 0 to 9. This results in the output shown here:

```
#Output of the circumference of each node

[0.0, 0.6283185307179586, 1.2566370614359172, 1.8849555921538759,
2.5132741228718345, 3.141592653589793, 3.7699111843077517,
4.39822971502571, 5.026548245743669, 5.654866776461628]
```

The next step is to extract the x and y coordinates. We can do this by using the code shown here:

```
#Extracting the x and y co-ordinates

x = [math.cos(circum) for circum in node_circumference]

y = [math.sin(circum) for circum in node_circumference]
```

This results in a list of x and y coordinates, as show in the code block here:

```
#Output of the x co-ordinates

[1.0, 0.8090169943749475, 0.30901699437494745, -0.30901699437494734,
-0.8090169943749473, -1.0, -0.8090169943749475, -0.30901699437494756,
0.30901699437494723, 0.8090169943749473]

#Output of the y co-ordinates

[0.0, 0.5877852522924731, 0.9510565162951535, 0.9510565162951536,
0.5877852522924732, 1.2246467991473532e-16, -0.587785252292473,
-0.9510565162951535, -0.9510565162951536, -0.5877852522924732]
```

Finally, we need to tie these coordinates together using a dictionary. We can do this by using the code shown here:

```
network_layout = dict(zip(node_points, zip(x, y)))
```

This results in a dictionary with a key, which is the node point (0 to 9), and the value, which is a tuple (*x*, *y*):

```
#Output of the dictionary

{0: (1.0, 0.0), 1: (0.8090169943749475, 0.5877852522924731), 2:
(0.30901699437494745, 0.9510565162951535), 3: (-0.30901699437494734,
0.9510565162951536), 4: (-0.8090169943749473, 0.5877852522924732), 5:
(-1.0, 1.2246467991473532e-16), 6: (-0.8090169943749475,
-0.587785252292473), 7: (-0.30901699437494756, -0.9510565162951535), 8:
(0.30901699437494723, -0.9510565162951536), 9: (0.8090169943749473,
-0.5877852522924732)}
```

Finally, we use the layout provider of the Bokeh package to render the network, in real time and in two-dimensional space:

```
#Output the network in two dimensional space

network.layout_provider = StaticLayoutProvider(graph_layout=network_layout)

plot.renderers.append(network)

output_file('network.html')
show(plot)
```

In the preceding code, the `StaticLayoutProvider` function is used to render the network that we built in a two-dimensional space, that is, the notebook or HTML file of the web page that the plot is finally rendered on.

Now that we have fully understood all the components that go into building a network, let's tie all the code together and view the resulting network:

```
#Import the required packages

import math
from bokeh.io import show, output_file
from bokeh.plotting import figure
from bokeh.models import GraphRenderer, StaticLayoutProvider, Oval

#Configure the number of nodes

total_nodes = 10
```

```
node_points = list(range(total_nodes))

#Create the network

plot = figure(x_range=(-1.1,1.1), y_range=(-1.1,1.1))

network = GraphRenderer()

#Customize your network

network.node_renderer.data_source.add(node_points, 'index')

network.node_renderer.glyph = Oval(height=0.2, width=0.3,
fill_color='blue')

network.edge_renderer.data_source.data = dict(start=[1]*total_nodes,
end=node_points)

#Render your network in 2-D space

node_circumference = [node*2*math.pi/10 for node in node_points]

x = [math.cos(circum) for circum in node_circumference]

y = [math.sin(circum) for circum in node_circumference]

network_layout = dict(zip(node_points, zip(x, y)))

#Output the network

network.layout_provider = StaticLayoutProvider(graph_layout=network_layout)

plot.renderers.append(network)

output_file('network.html')

show(plot)
```

This results in the network shown here:

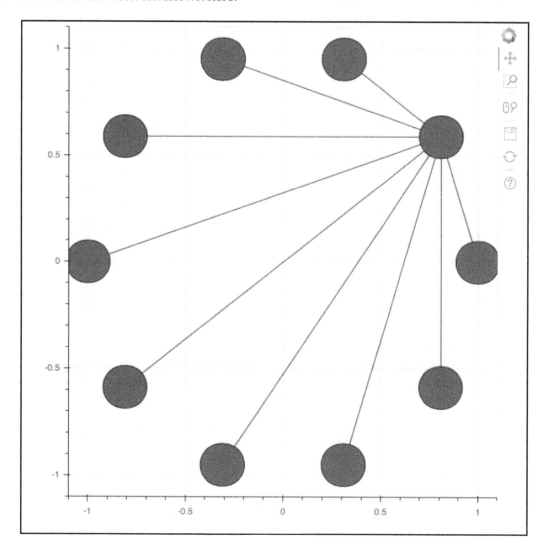

Visualizing networks with explicit paths

In this section, you will learn how to define a shape for the path that connects the two nodes of your network together.

The first step is to define a function that will return a quadratic path for us. In order to do this, we use the code shown here:

```
#Function that outputs the quadratic path

values = [value/100. for value in range(100)]

def quad_path(start, end, control, values):
    return [(1-value)**2*start + 2*(1-value)*value*control + value**2*end
for value in values]
```

`Values` is a list that contains a range of numbers from 0 to 0.99 which we will use to construct a function that mathematically returns a quadratic path based on the Bezier curve equation.

The function above takes in four arguments: `start`, `end`, `control`, and `values`. The start and endpoints define how the function will be displayed and constructed in two-dimensional space. The `quad_path` function then returns the x and y co-ordinates that are required to construct the quadratic network paths in two-dimensional space. To do this, we will make use of the same network layout that we used to construct the network in the previous subsection. This network layout is a dictionary that maps the node points to the x and y coordinates, and looks like this:

```
{0: (1.0, 0.0), 1: (0.8090169943749475, 0.5877852522924731), 2:
(0.30901699437494745, 0.9510565162951535), 3: (-0.30901699437494734,
0.9510565162951536), 4: (-0.8090169943749473, 0.5877852522924732), 5:
(-1.0, 1.2246467991473532e-16), 6: (-0.8090169943749475,
-0.587785252292473), 7: (-0.30901699437494756, -0.9510565162951535), 8:
(0.30901699437494723, -0.9510565162951536), 9: (0.8090169943749473,
-0.587785252292473)}
```

In order to build the `start` and `end`points, we use the code shown here:

```
#Initialize empty lists to store the x and y co-ordinates
x_point, y_point = [], []

#Store the starting and ending points

x_start, y_start = network_layout[0]

#Create the set of co-ordinates for the quadratic path
```

```
values = [value/100. for value in range(100)]
for node in node_points:
    x_end, y_end = network_layout[node]
    x_point.append(quad_path(x_start, x_end, 0, values))
    y_point.append(quad_path(y_start, y_end, 0, values))
```

In the preceding code, we first initialized empty lists to store the *x* and *y* coordinates. The starting points of the *x* and *y* coordinates were extracted from the network layout dictionary, and were 1.0 and 0.0 for x_start and y_start, respectively.

We then looped over the node points which are a list from 0 to 9, and then extracted the endpoints by subsetting the node points with the network layout. For instance, the endpoints of the second node would be:

```
network_layout[1] = (0.8090169943749475, 0.5877852522924731)
```

We then use the quad_path function to append the x and y points to the lists we initialized in the beginning.

The final step is just to add the new *x* and *y* coordinates to the network you created and render the plot. We can do this by using the code shown here:

```
#Add the x and y co-ordinates of the quadratic path to the network

network.edge_renderer.data_source.data['xs'] = x_point

network.edge_renderer.data_source.data['ys'] = y_point

#Output the plot

plot.renderers.append(network)

output_file("quad_path.html")

show(plot)
```

The final step is to tie all of this code together, along with the code that we used in the previous section, in order to build the network. This is illustrated in the code block shown here:

```
#Import the required packages

import math
from bokeh.io import show, output_file
from bokeh.plotting import figure
from bokeh.models import GraphRenderer, StaticLayoutProvider, Oval

#Configure the number of nodes

total_nodes = 10
node_points = list(range(total_nodes))

#Create the network

plot = figure(x_range=(-1.1,1.1), y_range=(-1.1,1.1))

network = GraphRenderer()

#Customize your network

network.node_renderer.data_source.add(node_points, 'index')

network.node_renderer.glyph = Oval(height=0.2, width=0.3,
fill_color='green')

network.edge_renderer.data_source.data = dict(start=[1]*total_nodes,
end=node_points)

#Render your network in 2-D space

node_circumference = [node*2*math.pi/10 for node in node_points]

x = [math.cos(circum) for circum in node_circumference]

y = [math.sin(circum) for circum in node_circumference]

network_layout = dict(zip(node_points, zip(x, y)))

network.layout_provider = StaticLayoutProvider(graph_layout=network_layout)

#Function that outputs the quadratic path

values = [value/100. for value in range(100)]
```

```python
def quad_path(start, end, control, values):
    return [(1-value)**2*start + 2*(1-value)*value*control + value**2*end
for value in values]

#Initialize empty lists to store the x and y co-ordinates
x_point, y_point = [], []

#Store the starting and ending points

x_start, y_start = network_layout[0]

#Create the set of co-ordinates for the quadratic path

values = [value/100. for value in range(100)]
for node in node_points:
    x_end, y_end = network_layout[node]
    x_point.append(quad_path(x_start, x_end, 0, values))
    y_point.append(quad_path(y_start, y_end, 0, values))
#Add the x and y co-ordinates of the quadratic path to the network

network.edge_renderer.data_source.data['xs'] = x_point

network.edge_renderer.data_source.data['ys'] = y_point

#Output the plot

plot.renderers.append(network)

output_file("quad_path.html")

show(plot)
```

This results in a network with a quadratic path connecting the nodes, as illustrated here:

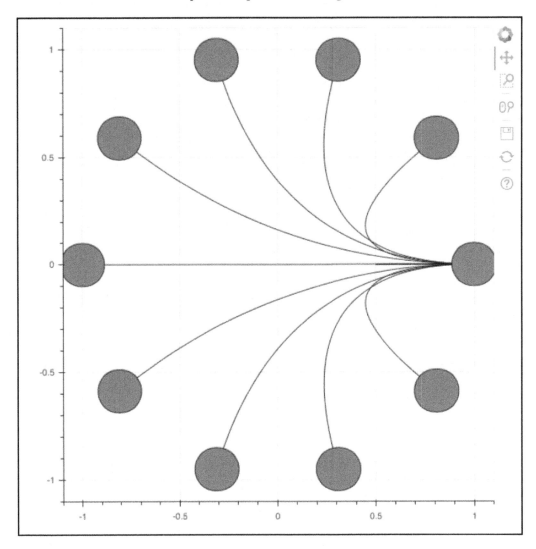

Visualizing geographic data with Bokeh

In this section, we are going to create a Bokeh visualization for the states in the USA that have the lowest crime rates. In order to do this, we will render a map of the USA and pinpoint the states that have the lowest crime rates.

The first step is to import the required packages:

```
from bokeh.sampledata import us_states
from bokeh.plotting import figure, show, output_file
from bokeh.models import HoverTool
```

`us_states` is a dictionary containing all the information that we need to construct a map of the USA in Bokeh. Additionally, if you wanted to create a map of any other country in Bokeh, you can find the necessary geo data on the web and import the file into your Jupyter Notebook.

The next step is to copy the data into Bokeh so that we can modify the data and delete states that are not significant (if required). Here, we will be deleting Hawaii and Alaska as we are only interested in the states in the mainland United States. We can delete individual states from the map by using the code shown here:

```
#Create a copy of the USA data in our notebook

usa_data = us_states.data.copy()

#Delete the states that are not of interest

del usa_data["HI"]
del usa_data["AK"]
```

The next step is to extract the `latitude` and `longitude` information from our data. We can do this by using the code shown here:

```
#Extract the latitude and longitude information

longitude = [usa_data[long]["lons"] for long in usa_data]

latitude = [usa_data[lat]["lats"] for lat in usa_data]
```

The next step is to design and configure how our plot should look. This can be done by using the code shown here:

```
#Create the figure

plot = figure(title="The 3 safest states in the USA")

#Configure the borders of the states

plot.patches(longitude, latitude, line_color="red", line_width=2)
```

In the preceding code, we use the patches function to construct blocks or patches according to the longitude and latitude coordinates that we built earlier. We give the borders of states a red color and a width of 2.

The next step is to create two lists that hold the longitude and latitude information of the three safest states in the USA. According to the popular website U.S. News, these states are Maine, Vermont, and New Hampshire.

The longitude and latitude of these three states are as follows:

```
#Longitude and latitude information for Maine

longitude = -69.44 West
latitude = 45.25 North

#Longitude and latitude information for Vermont

longitude = -72.57 West
latitude = 44.55 North

#Longitude and latitude information for New Hampshire

longitude = -71.57 West
latitude = 43.19 North
```

The next step is to put these location parameters into a list:

```
#Mapping the longitude and latitude information into lists

long_list = [-69.44, -72.57, -71.57]

lat_list = [45.25, 44.55, 43,19]
```

Finally, we define how we want mark these points on the plot by using the code shown here:

```
# Create the markers for the states

plot.diamond(long_list, lat_list, size=15, color='yellow')

# output the plot

output_file("safe.html")

show(plot)
```

One nice addition that we can add in order to enhance the interactivity of our plot is to create a hover tool and that gives us information about points of interest, such as latitude and longitude. We can create this tool by using the code shown here:

```
#Create the hover tooltip

hover_tool = HoverTool(tooltips = [
    ('Longitude', '@x'),
    ('Latitude', '@y')
])


#Embed the hover tool into the plot
plot = figure(title="The 3 safest states in the USA", tools = [hover_tool])
```

Finally, we can tie all the chunks of code together in order to create a geographic visualization of the three safest states in the USA:

```
#Import the required packages

from bokeh.sampledata import us_states
from bokeh.plotting import figure, show, output_file
from bokeh.models import HoverTool

#Create a copy of the USA data in our notebook

usa_data = us_states.data.copy()

#Delete the states that are not of interest

del usa_data["HI"]
del usa_data["AK"]

#Extract the latitude and longitude information
```

```
longitude = [usa_data[long]["lons"] for long in usa_data]

latitude = [usa_data[lat]["lats"] for lat in usa_data]

#Create the Hover Tool

hover_tool = HoverTool(tooltips = [
    ('Longitude', '@x'),
    ('Latitude', '@y')
])

#Create the figure

plot = figure(title="The 3 safest states in the USA", tools = [hover_tool])

#Configure the borders of the states

plot.patches(longitude, latitude, line_color="red", line_width=2)

#Mapping the longitude and latitude information into lists

long_list = [-69.44, -72.57, -71.57]

lat_list = [45.25, 44.55, 43,19]

# Create the markers for the states

plot.diamond(long_list, lat_list, size=15, color='yellow')

# output the plot

output_file("safe.html")

show(plot)
```

This results in the plot shown here:

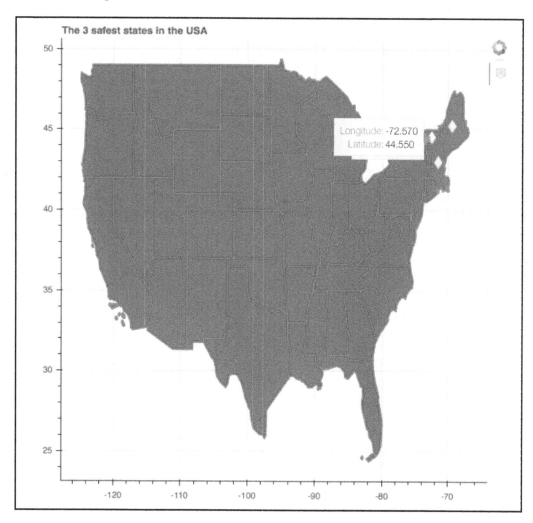

From this plot, we can identify a unique trend. We can immediately note how the safest states in the USA are very close to each other on the map. The added interactivity of the hover tool helps us extract the coordinates of these locations very quickly as well.

Using WebGL to improve performance

WebGL is a JavaScript API that is available in almost every popular browser in the market. Fundamentally, the Bokeh plots that are displayed on your browser do so with the help of plugins. This could slow down the rendering of plots, especially if the dataset that is used to render these plots is huge! WebGL renders plots using a GPU, without the need for plugins.

In order to enable WebGL while rendering plots, you simply need to use the code shown here while constructing the figure of the plot:

```
plot = figure(output_backend = 'webgl')
```

The only downside to rendering the plot in WebGL is that it does not support every component that Bokeh has to offer. At the moment, only two types of glyphs are supported with WebGL rendering. They are:

- Circle glyphs
- Line gyphs

The markers that are supported with WebGL are as follows:

- asterisk
- square
- diamond
- triangle
- inverted_triangle
- cross
- circle_cross
- square_cross
- diamond_cross
- x
- square_x
- circle_x

You can create a plot with all of Bokeh's components, but only the ones that are supported by WebGL will be rendered in WebGL, while the rest of the components will be rendered using plugins.

An example of rendering a plot using WebGL is shown here:

```
#Import required packages

import numpy as np
import random
from bokeh.io import output_file, show
from bokeh.plotting import figure

#Creating an array for the points along the x and y axes

array_x =np.array([1,2,3,4,5,6])

array_y = np.array([5,6,7,8,9,10])

#Creating a line plot

plot = figure(output_backend = 'webgl')

plot.line(array_x, array_y)

#Output the plot

output_file('numpy_line.html')

show(plot)
```

This results in the plot shown here:

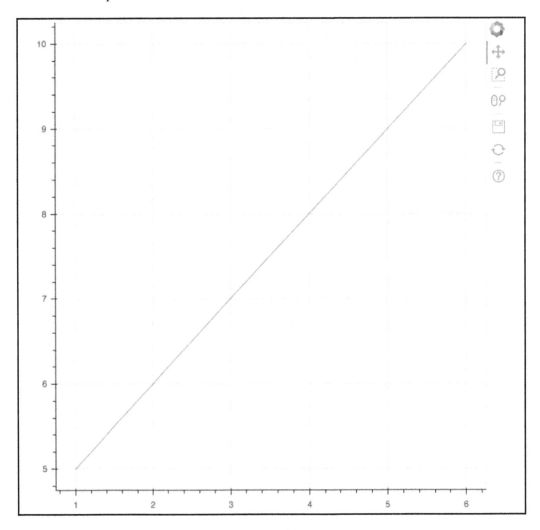

As you can clearly see, there is no visible difference between a plot rendered in BokehJS and a plot rendered using WebGL. The only time you will ever notice a difference is when you have a large dataset, in which case the speed of rendering will be much faster with WebGL.

The primary purpose of this section was to ensure that you had the knowledge required to improve the performance of the applications that you build using Bokeh. In most situations, you will render interactive visualizations of large volumes of data that can often render very slowly on a browser. WebGL helps alleviate this problem with a simple line of code.

Exporting plots as PNG images

The plot generated above looks both impressive and informative at the same time. We might want to publish this plot on a website or in a magazine/journal as a .PNG image with a higher level of quality. Luckily for us, Bokeh offers this flexibility.

Bokeh can generate such images by using the export function. This function uses a browser called Webkit to save the plot in its memory and capture a screenshot. The dimensions of the generated image will be the same as that of the plot you created.

The first step is to install a dependency that this Bokeh functionality depends upon. This is called Phantomjs. You can install this package using Anaconda with the command shown here:

```
conda install selenium phantomjs pillow
```

The next step is to install Selenium using `pip`. We can do this by using the command shown here:

```
pip3 install selenium
```

The final step is to export the plot that was created with the geographic data. We can do this by using the code shown here:

```
#Import the required packages

from bokeh.io import export_png

#Export the png image

export_png(plot, filename="safe_states.png")
```

The final image that is saved is shown here:

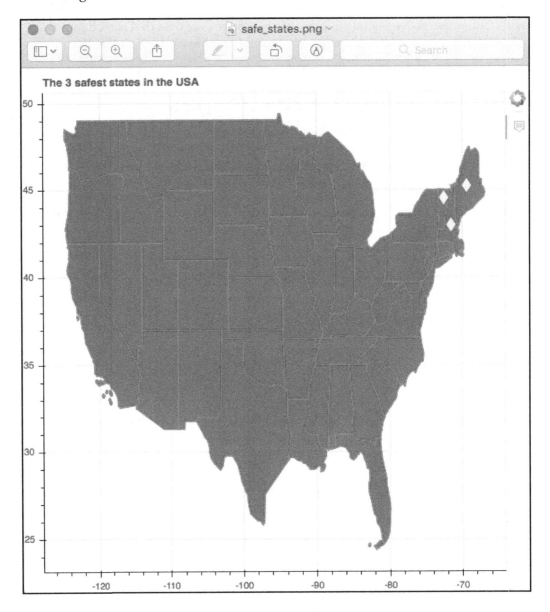

Summary

This chapter has given you a formal introduction into the world of constructing interactive networks using the Bokeh package. In a systematic way, you learned how to create and structure the process of building networks, both with the default straight path and the explicitly defined path.

You also learned how adding interactivity to geographical data can have a big impact on the viewer of your visualization, as he or she can now extract information from it.

Then, you learned how to use WebGL to render your plots faster and consequently improve the performance of your applications.

Finally, you learned about how you can export these plots in PNG format and render them at a very high quality for publishing.

In the next chapter, you will learn how to build your very own Bokeh application that you can use to analyze the stock market.

The Bokeh Workflow – A Case Study

8

When it comes to building your very own Bokeh visualization from scratch, a good practice to develop is to never start with Bokeh. Instead, the ideal approach is to perform a little exploratory analysis on your data first, in order to visualize the application you can create using Bokeh that can deliver the most value to your users.

Such an approach, of first exploring your dataset, helps you formulate the ideal visualization that you might want to present to your audience.

In this chapter, you will learn the exact workflow that you need to follow, from when you get the data to the final visualization that you want to present.

Bokeh, like most data visualization tools, is best used in a workflow that follows a logical sequence of steps, which will allow you to deliver impactful insights to your audience. This workflow can be summarized in four steps:

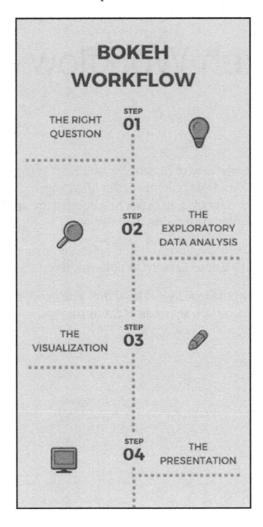

In this chapter, you will learn how to:

- Ask the right questions before visualizing your data
- Perform exploratory data analysis on a real dataset
- Build an interactive visualization that delivers specific insights
- Present your results

Technical requirements

You will be required to have Python installed on a system. Finally, to use the Git repository of this book, the user needs to install Git.

The code files of this chapter can be found on GitHub:
`https://github.com/PacktPublishing/Hands-on-Data-Visualization-with-Bokeh`.

Check out the following video to see the code in action:

`http://bit.ly/2sLSoX1`.

Asking the right question

Asking the right question is by far the most important step when it comes to data visualization. What is the answer that you are seeking?

Some of the most common questions that you need to ask yourself before deciding to visualize data are:

- Do I want to observe how well two features are correlated?
- Do I suspect potential outliers in my data that I cannot see unless I visualize my data?
- Do I want to see whether my data shows a particular trend over a period of time?
- Do I want to observe the distribution of individual features/columns in my data?
- Do I want to see whether there are clusters/groups within my data that I can potentially extract value from?
- Do I believe that a visualization can tell my audience a story about the data?

If the answer to any one of these questions is a yes, then you know that you need to visualize your data. The second question you want to ask yourself is, "What tool do I use to visualize my data?"

Some of the most common questions that you want to ask when deciding on a tool are:

- Do I want my audience to interact with my plots? If yes, Bokeh is a good choice, along with Tableau.
- Do I want to do exploratory data analysis and nothing else? If yes, Matplotlib and Seaborn in Python are good choices.

- Do I want to publish my plots in a publication that will be read by a wide audience? If yes, Bokeh is a good choice, along with Tableau.

Once you have decided that data visualization is a must and you have decided on the tool that you are going to use, the next step is to ask the right question about the data that you currently have. Let's have a look at the kinds of questions we can ask about the stock that we worked with throughout the course of the book:

- Is there a correlation between the high and low prices of particular stocks or multiple stocks?
- How do the opening prices of Apple's stock vary over time?
- Is there a similarity in the behavior of technology-based stocks such as Microsoft, Apple, and Google?

Your visualizations are only as good as the data that you have with you. If the quality of your data is bad, then your visualizations will suffer along with it. Some of the steps that you could take to improve the quality of your data are as follows:

- Create new features based on existing features that can better enhance your visualizations
- Merge multiple datasets together, which can help reveal better insights
- Deal with null values in a meaningful way
- Investigate the way the data was collected

These steps will drastically improve the quality of your presentations by revealing insights that were not available in the raw dataset itself.

Once we have a clear picture of the questions that we want answered, we can move on to the next step.

The exploratory data analysis

Since we have worked extensively with the **S&P 500 stock data** from Kaggle, we are going to be using that dataset in order to create our application. The dataset can be found here: https://www.kaggle.com/camnugent/sandp500/data.

The first step is to read the data into Jupyter Notebook and understand what the data looks like. This can be done using the code shown here:

```
#Import packages
```

```
import pandas as pd

#Read the data into the notebook

df = pd.read_csv('all_stocks_5yr.csv')

#Extract information about the data

df.info()
```

This renders the output shown in this screenshot:

```
<class 'pandas.core.frame.DataFrame'>
RangeIndex: 619040 entries, 0 to 619039
Data columns (total 7 columns):
date        619040 non-null object
open        619029 non-null float64
high        619032 non-null float64
low         619032 non-null float64
close       619040 non-null float64
volume      619040 non-null int64
Name        619040 non-null object
dtypes: float64(4), int64(1), object(2)
memory usage: 33.1+ MB
```

This sheds information on the number of rows the dataset has, the data types of each column, the number of variables, and any missing values.

The next step is to understand the kind of information contained in all the columns of your dataset. We can do this by using the code shown here:

```
df.head()
```

This results in the output shown here:

	date	open	high	low	close	volume	Name
0	2013-02-08	15.07	15.12	14.63	14.75	8407500	AAL
1	2013-02-11	14.89	15.01	14.26	14.46	8882000	AAL
2	2013-02-12	14.45	14.51	14.10	14.27	8126000	AAL
3	2013-02-13	14.30	14.94	14.25	14.66	10259500	AAL
4	2013-02-14	14.94	14.96	13.16	13.99	31879900	AAL

We can quickly see that we have the **date**, which is a time series attribute. **open, high, low,** and **close** are continuous numerical data and can be used to generate scatter plots. **volume** is also continuous, but the value is much larger than the other four numerical columns, and **Name** is a categorical column with the name of each stock.

Since **Name** is a categorical column with the name of each stock, it might be useful to understand the total number of categories the variable has. We can do this by using the code shown here:

```
df['Name'].value_counts()
```

This results in the output shown here:

```
DHR      1243
IQV      1197
COTY     1173
FOX      1169
NWSA     1169
FOXA     1169
NWS      1169
ALLE     1063
GOOG      975
NAVI      960
INFO      917
SYF       888
CFG       850
QRVO      781
WRK       662
PYPL      655
KHC       655
HPE       581
HPQ       581
CSRA      561
WLTW      528
UA        464
FTV       404
EVHC      297
HLT       276
DXC       215
BHGE      152
BHF       143
DWDP      109
APTV       44
Name: Name, Length: 505, dtype: int64
```

We now understand that there are 505 companies that are listed in the stock data.

Creating an insightful visualization

Now that we have a fundamental idea of what our data contains, we can proceed to making the visualization. The first step is to ensure we have the foundation of the visualization ready.

Creating the base plot

The foundation consists of the base plot that you want to visualize. In our case, we want to see how the volume of stocks traded over a period of time correlates with the high prices. In order to build this application, we use the code shown here:

```
#Import the required packages

from bokeh.io import curdoc
from bokeh.models import ColumnDataSource
from bokeh.plotting import figure
import pandas as pd

#Read the data into the notebook

df = pd.read_csv('all_stocks_5yr.csv')

#Convert the date column to a datetime object and extract the year only.

df['date'] = pd.to_datetime(df['date']).apply(lambda x:x.strftime('%Y'))

#Create the ColumnDataSource Object

data = ColumnDataSource(data = {
    'high' : df[df['date'] == '2013'].high,
    'low' : df[df['date'] == '2013'].low,
    'open' : df[df['date'] == '2013'].open,
    'close': df[df['date'] == '2013'].close,
    'volume': df[df['date'] == '2013'].volume,
    'Name' : df[df['date'] == '2013'].Name
})

#Specify the range of the x and y axis

xmin, xmax = min(df.high), max(df.high)
ymin, ymax = min(df.volume), max(df.volume)

#Create the plot
```

```
plot = figure(title = 'Volume traded Vs. High Prices', plot_height = 400,
plot_width = 700, x_range = (xmin, xmax),
            y_range = (ymin, ymax))

plot.diamond(x = 'high', y = 'volume', source = data)

plot.xaxis.axis_label = 'High Prices for 2013'

plot.yaxis.axis_label = 'Volume traded in 2013'

#Add the plot to the application

curdoc().add_root(plot)

curdoc().title = 'Volume and High prices of stocks'
```

In the preceding code, we first read in the data and stored it in a dataframe called `df`. In the next line, we converted the `date` column into a `datetime` object. We used the `apply` function in order to convert every element in the date column to the year format, which is `2011`, `2012`, and so on. The `lambda` function was used to apply this change in format to the dates across each element of the date column.

We then created a column data source element, in which we filtered each column of the dataframe based on the data from the year 2013 only. For example, the `high` column, which represents the high prices for the stocks, will only have data from the year 2013.

Finally, we specified the ranges for the *x*-and *y*-axes, and created a simple scatter plot between volume traded and high prices.

After saving the preceding script as `bokeh.py`, we can launch it by using the command shown here:

```
bokeh serve --show bokeh.py
```

This results in the application shown in this screenshot:

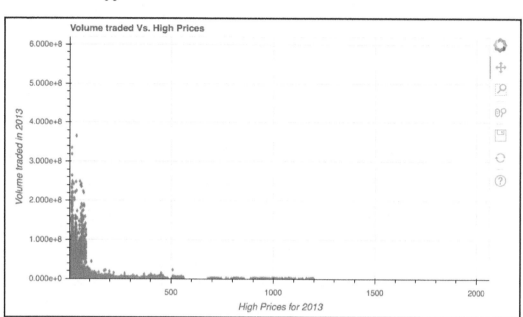

We can already see that there is a relationship between the volume of stocks traded and high prices. It seems that stocks that have a very high price are traded with much less frequency than stocks with a lower `high` price.

Mapping tech stocks

Now, if we were interested in investing and buying a few stocks from a technology giant—Google, Facebook, Amazon, Microsoft, or Apple—we might want to know how these companies performed compared to the rest of the companies in the S&P 500 index.

This can be implemented by using the code shown here:

```
#Import the required packages

from bokeh.io import curdoc
from bokeh.models import ColumnDataSource, CategoricalColorMapper
from bokeh.plotting import figure
from bokeh.palettes import Spectral5
import pandas as pd

#Read the data into the notebook
```

```python
df = pd.read_csv('all_stocks_5yr.csv')

df['date'] = pd.to_datetime(df['date']).apply(lambda x:x.strftime('%Y'))

#List the tech giants

tech_giants = ['GOOGL', 'FB', 'MSFT', 'AMZN', 'AAPL']

#Create the color map

color_map = CategoricalColorMapper(factors = tech_giants, palette = 
Spectral5)

#Create the ColumnDataSource Object

data = ColumnDataSource(data = {
    'high' : df[df['date'] == '2013'].high,
    'low' : df[df['date'] == '2013'].low,
    'open' : df[df['date'] == '2013'].open,
    'close': df[df['date'] == '2013'].close,
    'volume': df[df['date'] == '2013'].volume,
    'Name' : df[df['date'] == '2013'].Name
})

#Create ranges for the x and y axis

xmin, xmax = min(df.high), max(df.high)
ymin, ymax = min(df.volume), max(df.volume)

#Create the plot

plot = figure(title = 'Volume traded Vs. High Prices', plot_height = 400,
plot_width = 700, x_range = (xmin, xmax),
            y_range = (ymin, ymax))

plot.diamond(x = 'high', y = 'volume', source = data, color = dict(field = 
'Name', transform = color_map))

plot.xaxis.axis_label = 'High Prices for 2013'

plot.yaxis.axis_label = 'Volume traded in 2013'

#Add the plot to the application

curdoc().add_root(plot)

curdoc().title = 'Volume and High prices of stocks'
```

We then launch the application by using the command shown here in the Terminal/Shell:

```
bokeh.serve --show bokeh.py
```

This results in the application shown here:

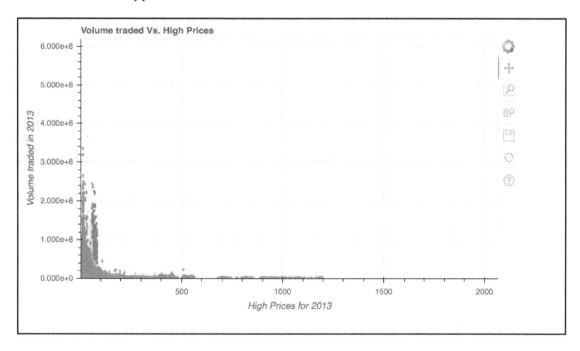

Now, we can clearly see where the tech giants are in terms of volume and high prices.

Adding a hover tool

The next step is to add a hover tool in order help us identify the names of the companies accurately as we interact with the visualization. We can do this by using the code shown here:

```
#Import the required packages

from bokeh.io import curdoc
from bokeh.models import ColumnDataSource, CategoricalColorMapper
from bokeh.plotting import figure
from bokeh.palettes import Spectral5
import pandas as pd
from bokeh.models import HoverTool
```

```
#Read the data into the notebook

df = pd.read_csv('all_stocks_5yr.csv')

df['date'] = pd.to_datetime(df['date']).apply(lambda x:x.strftime('%Y'))

#List the tech giants

tech_giants = ['GOOGL', 'FB', 'MSFT', 'AMZN', 'AAPL']

#Create the color map

color_map = CategoricalColorMapper(factors = tech_giants, palette =
Spectral5)

#Create the ColumnDataSource Object

data = ColumnDataSource(data = {
    'high' : df[df['date'] == '2013'].high,
    'low' : df[df['date'] == '2013'].low,
    'open' : df[df['date'] == '2013'].open,
    'close': df[df['date'] == '2013'].close,
    'volume': df[df['date'] == '2013'].volume,
    'Name' : df[df['date'] == '2013'].Name
})

#Create ranges for the x and y axis

xmin, xmax = min(df.high), max(df.high)
ymin, ymax = min(df.volume), max(df.volume)

#Create the hover tool

hover_tool = HoverTool(tooltips = [('Company:', '@Name')])

#Create the plot

plot = figure(title = 'Volume traded Vs. High Prices', plot_height = 400,
plot_width = 700, x_range = (xmin, xmax),
            y_range = (ymin, ymax))

plot.diamond(x = 'high', y = 'volume', source = data, color = dict(field =
'Name', transform = color_map))

#Adding the hover tool to the plot

plot.add_tools(hover_tool)
```

```
plot.xaxis.axis_label = 'High Prices for 2013'

plot.yaxis.axis_label = 'Volume traded in 2013'

#Add the plot to the application

curdoc().add_root(plot)

curdoc().title = 'Volume and High prices of stocks'
```

We can now launch this application by using the command shown here in the Terminal/Shell:

bokeh serve --show bokeh.py

Zooming into the application and using the hover tool, we get information about the name of the stock in the visualization, as shown here:

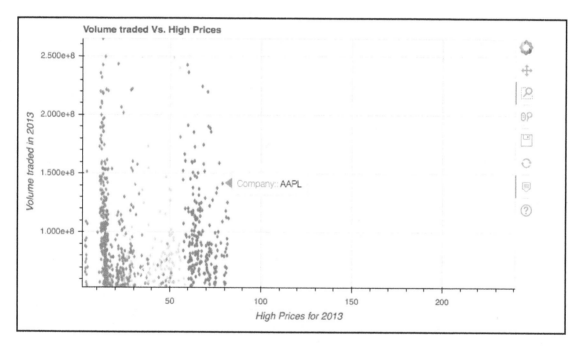

The zoom tool is the second tool under the Bokeh logo in the top-right corner. This is one of the default tools that is published by Bokeh in every visualization you create.

Improving performance using WebGL

The final step in creating a Bokeh visualization that renders quickly is to use WebGL in order to improve its performance. We can do this using the code shown here:

```
#Import the required packages

from bokeh.io import curdoc
from bokeh.models import ColumnDataSource, CategoricalColorMapper
from bokeh.plotting import figure
from bokeh.palettes import Spectral5
import pandas as pd
from bokeh.models import HoverTool

#Read the data into the notebook

df = pd.read_csv('all_stocks_5yr.csv')

df['date'] = pd.to_datetime(df['date']).apply(lambda x:x.strftime('%Y'))

#List the tech giants

tech_giants = ['GOOGL', 'FB', 'MSFT', 'AMZN', 'AAPL']

#Create the color map

color_map = CategoricalColorMapper(factors = tech_giants, palette =
Spectral5)

#Create the ColumnDataSource Object

data = ColumnDataSource(data = {
    'high' : df[df['date'] == '2013'].high,
    'low' : df[df['date'] == '2013'].low,
    'open' : df[df['date'] == '2013'].open,
    'close': df[df['date'] == '2013'].close,
    'volume': df[df['date'] == '2013'].volume,
    'Name' : df[df['date'] == '2013'].Name
})

#Create ranges for the x and y axis

xmin, xmax = min(df.high), max(df.high)
ymin, ymax = min(df.volume), max(df.volume)

#Create the hover tool
```

```
hover_tool = HoverTool(tooltips = [('Company:', '@Name')])

#Create the plot

plot = figure(title = 'Volume traded Vs. High Prices', plot_height = 400,
plot_width = 700, x_range = (xmin, xmax),
            y_range = (ymin, ymax), output_backend = 'webgl')

plot.diamond(x = 'high', y = 'volume', source = data, color = dict(field =
'Name', transform = color_map))

#Adding the hover tool to the plot

plot.add_tools(hover_tool)

plot.xaxis.axis_label = 'High Prices for 2013'

plot.yaxis.axis_label = 'Volume traded in 2013'

#Add the plot to the application

curdoc().add_root(plot)

curdoc().title = 'Volume and High prices of stocks'
```

Execute the script using the command shown here:

```
bokeh serve --show bokeh.py
```

You will notice a difference in the speed of execution. Your visualization will now render faster thanks to you using WebGL to enhance the performance of Bokeh!

Presenting your results

The right visualization is not just limited to picking the right type of plot, such as scatter plots or bar charts. It extends to picking the right colors, shapes, markers, and features.

Some of the questions that you will want to ask yourself when choosing the right visualization are as follows:

- Do I want to transmit a positive message to my readers? If yes, the colors green and blue are a great choice
- Do I want to transmit an alarming/negative message, indicating some form of danger/decline to my readers? If yes, the color red works best
- Do I want to show how two different segments/categories differ from each other? If yes, using contrasting colors such as red and blue works well

The tone of the insight and message that you want to convey is critical when it comes to creating the ideal visualization.

Summary

In this chapter, you learned how to build a real-time Bokeh visualization that can be used to analyze the performance of stocks from scratch. You learned how to perform initial exploratory data analysis in order to determine the kind of visualization that you wanted to create. You then created the visualization and improved its performance using WebGL.

Finally, you learned the four steps that form an integral part of the Bokeh workflow. You learned how asking the right kinds of questions is pivotal in any data visualization project, followed by the exploratory data analysis. You also learned how presenting your results is not limited to the type of plot you use, but also the tone of the message that you want to convey to the audience.

This concludes the book! I hope the book has given you an informative, hands-on introduction to the world of Bokeh! I hope you will continue to build on the skills you have learned here and produce interactive plots that can enthrall a wide audience!

Other Books You May Enjoy

If you enjoyed this book, you may be interested in these other books by Packt:

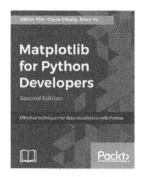

Matplotlib for Python Developers - Second Edition
Aldrin Yim, Claire Chung, Allen Yu

ISBN: 978-1-78862-517-3

- Learn how to clean your data and ready it for analysis
- Implement the popular clustering and regression methods in Python
- Train efficient machine learning models using decision trees and random forests
- Visualize the results of your analysis using Python's Matplotlib library
- Use Apache Spark's MLlib package to perform machine learning on large datasets

matplotlib Plotting Cookbook
Alexandre Devert

ISBN: 978-1-84951-326-5

- Discover how to create all the common plots you need
- Enrich your plots with annotations and sophisticated legends
- Take control of your plots and master colors, linestyle, and scales
- Add a dimension to your plots and go 3D
- Integrate your graphics into your applications
- Automate your work and generate a large batch of graphics
- Create interactive plots with matplotlib
- Combine your plots to create sophisticated visualizations

Leave a review - let other readers know what you think

Please share your thoughts on this book with others by leaving a review on the site that you bought it from. If you purchased the book from Amazon, please leave us an honest review on this book's Amazon page. This is vital so that other potential readers can see and use your unbiased opinion to make purchasing decisions, we can understand what our customers think about our products, and our authors can see your feedback on the title that they have worked with Packt to create. It will only take a few minutes of your time, but is valuable to other potential customers, our authors, and Packt. Thank you!

Index

Made in the USA
Coppell, TX
26 November 2020